STAR CHILDREN TEACH EARTH TRANSCENDENCE

Rita Comp, M.A.

CONTENTS

ACKNOWLEDGEMENTS

Grateful acknowledgement is made for permission to publish excerpts from:

THE CRYSTAL CHILDREN, 2003, CD/INDIGO, CRYSTAL AND RAINBOW CHILDREN, 2010, THE CARE AND FEEDING OF INDIGO AND CRYSTAL CHILDREN, 2010, Doreen Virtue, Hay House, NY.

PRONOIA IS THE ANTIDOTE FOR PARANOIA, 2009, Rob Brezsny, North Atlantic Books, Berkeley, CA.

CHILDREN AS TEACHERS OF PEACE, 1983, Gerald Jampolsky, M.D. (Ed.) Celestial Arts Publishers, Millbrae, CA.

BEHIND EVERY CLOUD THERE'S A RAINBOW, Gerald Jampolsky, M.D., 1982 Celestial Arts Publishers, Millbrae, CA.

NEW WAYS IN DISCIPLINE, Dorothy M. Baruch, Ph.D, McGraw Hill Book Co., New York NY.

I KNOW YOU LOVE ME, Caroline Schneider, Joy Publications, P.O. Box 373, Santa Maria, CA.

ESP Class Tapes, Jane Roberts (author of the Seth Literature). Special excerpts on dream material for use in classes, conferences and seminars.

LONELINESS AND LOVE, 1972 Clark Moustakas, Prentice-Hall, Englewood Cliffs, NJ.

DEDICATION

To the creative and innovative spirits of those

responsible adults, - - parents and teachers who are

dedicated to protecting the divine spirit within their

 children and who are determined to energize a more

harmonious, life affirming probability for them and for

all species.

PREFACE

Our planet abounds with paradigm shifts or rapid changes which can sometimes seem overwhelming. The purpose and intent of this book is blessed and guided by angels and/or spirit guides as disclosed by the many miracles and solutions that occurred with its development. We have guardian angels, many teachers and guides that want to shower us with blessings as demonstrated in these pages. They bring an awareness of a much needed change that is long overdue in our educational system that will prevent needless transitional suffering and burnout to parents and teachers and our "New Children" with the beneficent gifts they bring. It is time to acknowledge, listen to, and adapt curriculum to these beings of higher abilities. The awareness of relating holistically with our young people, protecting and encouraging their creative or inner divinity is crucial.

KRYON of Ashtar Command enlightens: "Your children, the children of now that have come to the earth to assist in the process of ascension are the ones manifesting a lot of light and love into your reality by anchoring that light and love into the hearts of each and every being that they come into contact with ethereally, consciously and subconsciously. In order to help them remain in this new type of frequency that they carry within them, we have instituted many teachers, who are secretly and unbeknownst to your government, communicating with your children now on a cellular level in the language of the heart.

"Each school on your planet has been supplied with such teachers, and they will know precisely who and what they are. They are a special class of teachers in your schools present for a brief time. These are what you call a 'substitue teacher'. Yes indeed, dear ones, we come to your children at precise moments to put forth the information that they are in need of and to show them not to be afraid of anything. And so these teachers are touching on topics that others simply do not want to mention.

"They are sending these children home filled with love and light. They are reminding the children of who they are, constantly keeping their vibrations high. And these children of NOW know exactly who they are, since they are not plagued by the veil of forgetfulness. And just as many of you have experienced, as light workers, there are still obstacles that they must cope with.

"Each child that comes into your world now is a star seed. These children are literally the future generation of hybrid beings—a mixed origin from the celestian spheres and of humanity. They are going to be confronted by anything the human ego can throw at them.

"Many of you who are now helping the teachers are going to find that you are drawn to assist these children in order to keep their vibrations high. These children are no longer limited by a misconception of reality. These children remember who they are . They know why they have come onto this planet. They remember and know their missions, and they are free from the veil of forgetfulness.

"Whereas before, when you, as light workers had arrived on this planet, it was dangerous for us to step in and remind you of who you were/are until it was time. We have waited to find our own way, and have assisted you secretly from behind the veil. Now due to all of your efforts in assisting the earth and humanity, due to all the struggles you have gone through, each and every one of you, who had to wake up and break through the veil on your own – due to all this – it's now possible for us to see the children face to face – and help them."

We can prevent our escalating teen suicide rates by helping chioldren release their destructive negative feelings (See pg. 55 for the method.) When they release negative feelings of hurt, fear and anger, they feel and radiate the energies of happiness and love which drive their creations. Total acceptance of them as good and in a state of grace is the foundaton step for co-creating. Helping them maintain a balanced and happy state of mind is important to their understanding that they are in control of their emotions and feelings a well as what they create.

They need to transmute pain and remove the deeply rooteed blocks of anger and hatred that impact others and our beloved earth. Out thoughts and actions affect the weather and envronment. Dr. Masru Emoto, in his book THE HIDDEN MESSAGES IN WATER, shows how our thoughts and emotions as humans deeply impact the environment. Drought, earthquakes, typhoons and hurricanes have been documented by authors Corinne McLaughlin and Gordon Davidson in their article, THE EFFECT OF HUMAN THOUGHTS AND EMOTIONS ON WEATHER PATTERNS.

Hurts and pains are directly what interfere with the streams of energy being sent to their bodies and minds as well as their perceptions of such energies and the guidance sent by their higher consciousness.

This book illustrates that the restructuring of relationships with all children into warm, cooperative caring, with appropriate limits and boundaries provides the best climate for growth and continuing consciousness expansion. Such restructuring builds trust, wins cooperation and removes resistances to learning. It also demonstrates that consciousness expansion brings healthy survival.

CHAPTER 1

THE "NEW CHILDREN" TEACH TRANSCENDANCE

THE "NEW CHILDREN" are SUPER PSYCHIC CHILDREN, STAR CHILDREN and DNA CHANGING CHILDREN (To view these children and their amazing abilities visit You Tube, Super Psychic Children.)

Many teachers have come to realize that thousands of "New Children" are necessitating a long overdue change in outdated school curriculum with parents insisting children be taught how to develop and strengthen their psychic and intuitive skills. Some children and parents are seeking help in coping with these already enhanced psychic and intuitive abilities. (Visit You Tube/Developing Psychic Abilities to learn excellent exercises.)

These aware adults realize most public schools have not been meeting the needs of these children now demonstrating high sensitivity, heightened perceptions, greater intuition and outstanding psychic abilities. They also have a multi-dimensional awareness: they perceive a boader range of reality.

According to "Awakening –Healing News" from Keith Luke, "They perceive all at once, seeing all that is. They do not think within their mental structuring in linear form, but rather holographically. This type of thinking brings high intelligence. Their perceptive abilities are utilizing once dormant areas of brain matter that is coming alive with the genetic changes that are occurring at this time. Many of these beings are coming as starseeds to bring forward once again and carry the energies that must be utilized with the coming shift."

These children have an awareness of scientific, historical, anthropological and spiritual knowledge not consciously learned and sometimes called "knowledge bombs, which sometimes hurt". Mary Rodwell, author of AWAKENING , says an 8-year-old has called her downloading of information "knowledge bombs", as complex data conveyed through images and concepts that seem to create a heightened consciousness level. These 'starchildren' exhibit a maturity and wisdom beyond their years." Among the many gifts they bring to us, they manifest unusual art work, languages and scripts, and they have multi-dimensional healing abilities, and a healing DNA.

ABC News' Diane Sawyer has also explored the issue of these extraordinary children in a November 2005 interview with an entire family of Indigo Children. Sawyer said that "this phenomenon was fascinating and was across the country."

UCLA researchers have discovered children are being born with a New DNA that makes them immune to all illness. They first discovered this in the Indigo children and note it is now also spreading "vibrationally" and rapidly to adults. There are now 60 million people worldwide with this new DNA as UCLA continues to monitor it.

Drunvalo Melchizedek, author of THE SERPENT OF LIGHT: BEYOND 2012, has been following these children for two years and rejoicing in the many gifts they have come to share with us. He says "These kids know exactly what you're feeling and what you're thinking. You can't hide anything from them. It's really amazing. I see it as a phenomenon like the ET's except they aren't coming here in spaceship form—they are coming here in spirit form, making it personal, by coming into the earth's evolutionary cycle and joining with us." (Visit his experiences on You Tube.)

These children set us special tasks and new learning experiences. Many of their behaviors call for parents and teachers to change their treatment and upbringing of these children to avoid destroying their precious abilities and assist them in bestowing their gifts as teachers to us all. Fortunately, some educators with foresight have taken steps to accommodate these advanced children with programs tailored to their needs.

NEW EDUCATIONAL PROGRAMS

The INDIGOS have been challenging our schools and creating an educational crisis to show us that our educational system needed to adapt to their needs. One educator observed: "The education of the New Children requires careful consideration. These children - - especially the multi-talented and meta gifted children - - will simply not put up with a rigid and limited educational framework. They will develop more rapidly than the average child, reading sooner and questioning deeper and quicker, and they need a supportive framework in which this development can take place.

"We realize that specialist education will not be feasible for most parents and that many New Children have elected to be taught in mainstream education, hard as that may be for them at times. But they do have to learn to mix with mainstream kids. An Indigo can survive within conventional schooling but Rainbows, and especially Crystals, will not thrive in such a restrictive and over-controlling environment."

Wendy Chapman and Carolyn Flynn, visionary authors of THE COMPLETE IDIOT'S GUIDE TO INDIGO CHILDREN suggests these guidelines and progressive possibilities. "The schools are changing. With so many Indigos flooding the school systems now, it's interesting to note the number of programs developed to give children opportunities to develop more tolerance."

(Go to ESL.net/inservices/teaching_diversity.php, which lists 25 resources to teach about peace and tolerance.   Consult indigochild.com/schools. Html.)

CHARTER SCHOOLS are new, innovative public schools that operate independently of the mainstream system. Many of them adapt alternative educational philosophies such as Waldorf into the curriculum, taking the best and leaving the rest.

SUDBURY SCHOOLS . There are about 20 of these in the world. One experimental school, Sudbury Valley in Framingham, Massachusetts, has pioneered innovative practices that have earned the notice of the Indigo community. - - Children are naturally inclined to learn and take on the responsibility of learning. This style is for the very independent Indigo who shows an interest in leadership and responsibility. The belief that children learn best when they take responsibility for directing their learning is at the very heart of the unschooling movement. They do not have classes or textbooks... Children use teachers as resources.

MAGNET SCHOOLS focus on specific subjects or skills such as science, computers, art or theater - - if your child has a specific talent, that matches a nearby magnet school, this might be a great fit.

HOMESCHOOLING can offer a blend of the child-directed curriculum, with the freedom and flexibility to tailor the topics and style to the interest of the child. But homeschooling is only as good as the discipline and commitment of the parent who is teaching. – One of the biggest concerns of parents considering homeschooling is how the child will develop social skills. Many options exist for the child to participate in various school activities (See the COMPLETE IDIOT'S GIUIDE TO INDIGO CHILDREN, P.185)

GIFTED PROGRAMS: Many progressive public (and private) schools offer gifted programs that cultivate imaginativeness, creativity, entrepreneurship and collaboration. These enhance many of the Indigo gifts.

Expect to see MANY MORE SCHOOLS - - private, alternative and even public embrace curricula that develop the heart and spirit as a well as the mind and body. See the Consciousness-Based Education Assn., on the Internet. It is a non-profit resource that works with new and existing schools as well as after-school programs, to provide programs that help cultivate creativity and inner advancement in children. It also uses transcendental meditation.

To make the transition for these children easier, parents need to keep themselves informed and speak up regarding appropriate education and treatment of their children.

2012

Many observers and researchers believe the New Children come from all areas of the universe and carry a new vibration that will transform the consciousness of humanity. They have come to raise the vibration of Earth. These observers predict that on Winter Solstice, the human race will progress to a new level, described as the Fifth World. The New Children provide the basis for a whole new kind of human - - the Fifth Root Race. They believe there will be intelligent communication between human, mineral and animal life. Gems will increasingly be used for healing; all will have greater respect for plants and animals, and be more protective of the environment.

VIBRATIONAL SHARING: FOUR EVENTS

The Super Psychic Children of China are also demonstrating the power of their VIBRATION to pass on their abilities to others. Keith Varnum, in describing the Super Psychic Kids, notes that the "Chinese government officials discovered that when they have children who aren't psychic, socialize with the psychic children, the non-psychic children quickly absorb the ability to perform the same astounding feats as the psychic kids." It seems probable that the Crystal Children who communicate mind-to-mind will use this VIBRATIONAL manner to teach their parents psychic abilities.

Drunvalo Melchizadek also reveals, through UCLA Research, that 60 million people in the world changed their DNA to drastically improve their immune system against HIV infection through spontaneous genetic mutation. This DNA change is spreading rapidly, again, through the power of VIBRATION. (His full report is available on You Tube.)

Uri Geller demonstrated another amazing VIBRATIONAL feat on TV In the 70'S. He asked his viewing audience in Europe to place utensils in front of their TV sets. With millions watching, he bent the tableware in their homes. After the show, it was reported that over 1,500 children vibrationally absorbed this ability just by watching it once.

THE SACRED MISSIONS

Researchers and authors also foretell that these "Children of Oneness" are here to assist with the ascension of the planet; however, each group has a unique mission. Indigo Children ("System Busters") are toppling old systems that lack integrity, thereby clearing the path for Crystal Children.   Nikki Patillo, Indigo author of CHILDREN OF THE STARS: ADVICE FOR CHILDREN AND PARENTS, urges us to understand that "Indigos demonstrate our society is dysfunctional and needs to change to accommodate beings of higher ability."   Crystal Children will bring healing, peace and harmony and Rainbow Children will build on the foundation efforts of the Indigo and Crystal Children.

Numerous researchers and authors agree with her that it appears all the Star Children will collectively serve in helping humanity ascend "to a higher vibrational frequency.. . thousands of these souls are arriving as teachers and healers for the human race.- - -they will take us to the next level in our evolution and reveal to us inner and higher power. They function as a group consciousness rather than as individuals, and they live by the 'Law of One' or global oneness."

Doreen Virtue has reviewed hundreds of stories from parents and teachers about the Star Children. "As I reviewed these stories, I felt my heart swell with love and gratitude. Just reading the stories was like being in the presence of mighty angels! I felt ecstatically high by these amazing youngsters' presence on our planet."

SUPER PSYCHIC CHILDREN

China has discovered "Super Psychic Children" about 25 years ago (1986), within the same time frame as the arrival of the Indigo Children. By 1977,   100,000 of these children had been recognized and their numbers are increasing rapidly. They are worldwide, as Mary Rodwell, (author of "AWAKENING, How Extraterrestrial Contact Can Transform Your Life"), discovered from her connections with UFO's and as one writing extensively about these developments. "Families have contacted me from all over the globe, not only from Australia, Europe North and South America , but Asia and Russia, and all describe children and adults that exhibit transformative changes such as telepathy, clairvoyance and healing as they become more spiritually aware and begin to operate on a multi-dimensional band of reality. --- In the deep region of Himalayas, people are reporting strange behavior in children. The children are using sign languages which are unknown to their families and anyone around.."

She shares her 1999 experience with Inge Bardor from Mexico, who could read from her hands and her feet blindfolded. With her high-heeled shoes on, Inge was able to read the newspaper placed under her feet as if it was in her hands and she wasn't blindfolded. She also accepted photos from the audience, giving information describing the person. She has learned of 1000 psychics in Mexico City who can also read from various parts of their bodies: ears, hands, feet, nose, chin, tongue, in the same way the Super Psychic Children of China demonstrate.

Paul Dong and Thomas Rafill authored CHINA'S SUPER PSYCHICS, and explain how many millions have been spent researching Extra Human Function (EHF) in these children. Research schools are widespread throughout China.

Their EHF abilities have attracted the interest of science journals whose writers have come to witness and validate the authenticity of these demonstrations. There are many stories validated in their book. Some of these describe the childrens' abilities to do "psychic writing". This is a technique where they imagine some written words on a blank sheet of paper inside a pencil case. The case was opened later to disclose they had correctly projected the written words onto the paper.

When blindfolded, these children were able to see with their ears, nose, mouth, tongue, armpits, hands or feet. One demonstration included crumpling a printed page torn from a book, and placing it under the armpit of a child. The child read every word on the page accurately. On another awesome occasion, 1000 people were given a rosebud. A six-year-old child came on stage and with a wave of her hand, "willed" the 1000 rosebuds to blossom into beautiful roses.

Under the strict discipline of scientific research, the Chinese government has observed these children changing the human DNA molecule in a petri dish.

DNA CHANGING CHILDREN

Medical researchers at UCLA are discovering Indigo youngsters have a unique DNA pattern no one else has, with 24 active DNA codons instead of the usual 20. Many more children are being born with the new DNA. They have a remarkable resistance to illness and seem immune to every disease.   Further, they seem to be spreading it vibrationally ; UCLA's latest report was 60 million people or 1% of the planet now have the new DNA "CONTAGION". IN 2009 a 47% drop in AIDS occurred, the single largest drop of a single disease in the history of the world.

THE STAR CHILDREN

The Star Children have been arriving in three waves: the Indigo Children, The Crystal Children and the Rainbow Children, and/or the Golden Children. A few Indigo Scouts began arriving as far back as 100 years ago; more were born between the 1940's and 1960's. The first big wave came in the 1970's and these Indigos are now 35-25 years old. The second big wave came in the 1980's to late 1990's and they are 25-8 years old. The Crystal Children have been born in the late 90's through the present, and range from 8-0 years old. Rainbow Children were generally born in the year 2000 and above. It is estimated that 80% of all children born in 2011, are in one of these three groups, with the Crystal Children leading at 75% of newborns.

They are called by the names of colors observed in their auras. The Indigo Children have Indigo, deep blue or violet colored auras; the Crystal Children have opalescent auras, with beautiful multi-colors in pastel hues; the Rainbow Children have every color of the rainbow in their auras; the Golden Children have a golden aura.

Edgar Cayce predicted groups of amazing individuals would begin to incarnate on earth late in the twentieth century and beyond. These children would be categorized into three different groups: Indigo, Crystal and Rainbow, each having his or her own special gifts and talents. The book PSYCHIC CHILDREN: A SIGN OF OUR EXPANDING

AWARENESS, by Peggy Day and Susan Gale shows how these children can be recognized and nurtured as the special people they truly are. Cayce describes psychic children throughout the world including, the wonderful work various organizations in countries such as China, Mexico, Bulgaria, and Russia are doing to develop and use the psychic talents of their children. (From Carol Chapman's review for Amazon books.)

Arthur C. Clarke in his Sci-Fi Book CHILDHOOD'S END also predicted a new step in evolution brought to earth by the extra terrestrials (UFO) concerns to protect Planet Earth. It is similar to the changes now happening on Earth through our New Children, except Earth people will be allowed to keep their independence and creativity. They will teach us how to make better use of our abilities and further help us to develop our psychic abilities.

Dumari Dancoes illumines that "Our planet has reached a crisis of epic proportions. We as her children have reached a point of stagnation in our growth -- More and more of the world's people are becoming impoverished in both material and spiritual terms as a small minority accumulate more power and wealth for themselves. We continue to trash our planet in the name of development and to kill each other in senseless wars, often fought in the name of religion and freedom." The Star Children have come to make us realize what we are doing and why we need to change. They are shifting our consciousness to help us change.

"They have been sent here from all areas of the universe- - - These children will bring peace, topple corrupt systems, and shift dimensional consciousness in the years to come." They will help the planet move into the new energy of love and peace that includes integrity and cooperation.

Nikki Patillo urges parents, "Help your Star Children figure out what their life's purpose is and how they will contribute to humanity as a whole. You must help these special children understand and be unafraid of their gifts."

CRYSTAL CHILDREN

Each year's crop of Crystal Children born reveals increasingly profound spiritual abilities – We're progressing from an evolutionary standpoint. We won't rely so much on the spoken or written word; communication will be faster, more direct, and more honest because it will be mind-to mind. – These children will teach their parents how to develop and strengthen psychic abilities.--One child in the womb telepathically revealed her date of birth.

The first thing one notices is their enormous eyes with an intense stare; they have magnetic personalities that seem to scan one and read what that person is about. Crystal Children are very musically oriented; they may sing before talking. They are exceptionally gifted in art and music.

Dr. Doreen Virtue in her book THE CRYSTAL CHILDREN, explains how they will often discuss angels and spirit guides, and past life memories. "Haley said the Angel of Knowledge was working with her. She said the Angel teaches her reading and math. The Kindergarten teacher corroborated this, telling mom how impressed she was with Haley's vocabulary."

"Offering their love is the collective mission of Crystal Children. 12 week old Isabelle's energy is so strong and loving that she has an instant calming, peaceful effect on other people. Haley's mother says, 'Her hands on my shoulders make me calm.'

"They are fearless and impervious to fear and filled with great love. Mother says of her 18-month old daughter, 'Celeste is the sweetest, most loving spirit I've ever encountered. She goes right up to strangers, takes their hands, and you can just feel the love she's sending. A very sensitive, passionate, attentive person.'

"Six-year-old Robert wants to give something to every homeless person on the street. He has love for all people. He wants to comfort every person he sees in need.

"Crystal Children emanate love in all their actions and deeds. They're living examples of operating from the higher self and not the ego. They're indicators that the human race is evolving above petty differences and squabbles."

ANGELIC GUIDANCE

Doreen also brings an urgent message to parents about nurturing their children from the angels: "Listen well, parents of the nineties. You, too, have an exceedingly important mission to fulfill. You must ensure your children stay intuitive and they stay very close to nature. Don't push them to succeed at the expense of losing their soul purpose. For our purpose is our guiding force, and without direction, your child will feel lost, alone, and afraid.

"So much better for parents to focus their children on spiritual studies, as this is their true nourishment that will ensure their growth and survival. We angels are here to help you parents and we won't interfere or get in the way. Simply allow us to cast a new light on difficult situations, a task we complete with joy in our hearts, simply by your open invitation to allow us to heal. Do not ever feel that God doesn't hear your prayers, for he sends us to your side the instant that you call."

Doreen Virtue also describes the role of grandparents. "The souls of Crystal Children were obviously selecting parents who could raise them in a spiritually nurturing environment. Occasionally I met parents who were spiritually unaware. In these cases their grandparents were highly evolved light workers who helped protect and hone the child's spiritual knowledge and gifts. Most people told me that their Crystal child was a profound spiritual teacher who taught parents a great deal about being an exceptionally loving and kind person."

She states on her new CD, INDIGO, CRYSTAL AND RAINBOW CHILDREN that she has channeled Mother Mary urging us to realize that - - -"Mother love is very crucial now. There is a crying need for mothers to speak up! In our global family, mother's know what to do, and need to own mother energy now." She assures that this effort would speed up the transition.

The Indigo Children have come to also prepare a path for the Crystal Children. The first wave of Indigo or warrior children want to cut down anything that lacks integrity, whether it is government, healthcare, education or legal systems. They can sense dishonesty and know when they're being lied to or manipulated. They are called the "System Busters", as their mission indicates.

One grandmother states, "My granddaughter who just turned four may be an Indigo Child. She is not exposed to advanced tech and does not watch regular TV. She speaks and writes Spanish and has worked with a tutor for a year now. She has a knowing that would blow your mind away. She talks about her life as Martha.

"She has the comprehension of an adult and comes up with things that I can only think come from the collective consciousness. My daughter does give her many advantages. She is in a special school now for advanced children. They study science, astronomy and do experiments.   This school is not about fun and games. She has the quest for knowledge and has a memory that is unbelievable."

Actually this child sounds more like a Cusp Child, who has the characteristics of both the Crystal Child and Indigo, but is predominantly a Crystal Child.   She does not have the fiery temperament of an Indigo, and is not giving anyone the kind of problems typical of the Indigo's frustration.

When my newborn granddaughter, Avery, arrived in April, 2011, she announced herself as a Crystal Child as she was taken, in a C-section from her mother's womb and placed on her mother's chest. She propped herself up on her arms, lifted her head up without any support and greeted mom with a big smile.   According to "Child Development" on the internet, these motor skills do not occur until the age of four months.

She has typical enormous eyes and radiates soothing, comforting, healing vibrations from the pictures I have on my wall at eye level,--I especially feel the beautiful benefits when I roll over in my bed, look into her eyes, and get ready to sleep. I couldn't understand how this was possible until I checked it on the internet. I found that Pythagoras had explained, "Everything is in a state of vibration. Love energy has a 'pi' vibration. It heals."

The VIBRATION MAGAZINE BLOG explains that "anyone who looks attentively at the photo of a plant can derive some of the benefits to such attunements." The authors also explored their spiritual and healing connection to the plants. I realized that if we could get benefits from a photo of a plant, we could surely get the typical Crystal loving vibrations from the photo of a Crystal child.

On my first meeting with her at the age of three months, she stared into my eyes with a knowing smile and seemed to know me. Telepathically, I gave her fullness of Universal and unconditional love, and told her I knew she was a Crystal Star Child, and had an important mission. Her mother took photos of this joyful meeting which serves as a constant reminder of gratitude for Avery's choice to be with us and to share in her gifts. Her name, Avery, means "magical counsel", and the family senses she is here to do plenty of this. At the same time she extends to us the opportunity of a new awareness and education in taking responsibility to help protect her magical counsel gifts.

See page 16, THE CARE AND FEEDING OF INDIGO CHILDREN, for the angels directions in nurturing, as channeled through Doreen Virtue. We are urged to "insure our children stay intuitive, and stay very close to nature" and to "focus them on spiritual studies as this is their true nourishment."

Avery is transformed by music. It brings lots of smiles and joy as she holds onto my little finger when I mimic conducting a Mozart theme. She has a Mozart cubed music box which plays different instruments according to the side that is pushed, and she is eagerly learning to do this. Typical of Crystal children, she is very musically oriented.

Dr. Barbara Lane is a hospital hypno-therapist gifted in channeling . She has been a long time friend of 32 years and her predictions about our lives invariably come true.   About Avery, she says, "She definitely is a Crystal Child and very brilliant. Her main interests are in Science and Creativity. She is a new blend of modern day healing, using not only vibrational healing but also the traditional roles of doctor/nurse. She will be respected as a blend of both worlds. Dr. Lane was not aware of the following information about the Crystal Child's very powerful healing gifts, when she channeled this information.

In contrast to the Indigos, the Crystal children are called "The Peacemakers" because they are blissful and even tempered—happy, delightful and forgiving, and are advocates for love and peace on the planet. They have a higher group consciousness than the Indigo. They are very powerful children, here as soothers and healers, and can do long distance healing. Their eyes are large, wise and penetrating beyond their years. Most parents   describe the child as "an angel" with whom they have a very happy relationship. They are very sensitive, warm and -caring.

They know at once whether someone is lying to them and what is in her/his heart. When they perceive this, they will just step back, as if to signal the communication is ended.

Doreen Virtue has just released a guide to this new generation of highly sensitive young people on a 2-CD set called INDIGO, CRYSTAL

AND RAINBOW CHILDREN (Hay House, May 2005). She describes the Rainbow Children as "the embodiment of our divinity and the example of our potential. They have never lived on this planet before. They're entirely fearless of everybody. They're little avatars who are all about service.- - -"

Others who have met them describe their experience as, "It's like sitting before a Master." Elsewhere Doreen Virtue comments, "Their energy is the purest so far, they have a vibration of complete joy and contentment, have a peaceful nature, and their presence gives out a feeling of holiness."

CHARACTERISTICS OF INDIGO CHILDREN

The anger and frustration of the Indigos occur because they have a strong sense of mission that includes complex ideas of achieving big changes in government, environment and society, and health care.

They have found fulfillment of their mission as "system busters" by globally leading the Occupy Movement.   Professer Al-Majma Zidjaly, in Oman, has dubbed this action a "youthquake", noting it is primarily led by the young. They have been determined   to reduce homelessness, joblessness and poverty, and have seized upon this opportunity.   SaLuSa of The Galactic Federation of Light describes their courage in playing a big role in this forward movement of the "Law of Oneness."

"Many of the Indigo Children are now old enough to bring their talent into play, and have a very high level of wisdom to share. However, such advanced souls rarely speak of their abilities, but go about their work with hardly being noticed.

"Not everyone likes the idea of demonstrating , but it is the type of energy that is found with the younger generations who are fearless where it is concerned. They are the ones who understand that the old ways are no longer acceptable, and will continue their protests until they achieve success. Many are those souls who have incarnated for this purpose but also carry the answers to the problems, having higher levels of consciousness than most people. These Indigo youth have average IQ's of around 130, but many are in the genius range of 160 or higher."

Many of the inter-net savvy youth have increasingly, over the years, been viewing autocrats and absolute monarchies as anachronisnms. The revolts of Arab Spring were especially caused by a large percentage of educated but dissatisfied youth refusing to accept the status quo.

The idea for large demonstrations spread throughout the planet and were promoted by computer-literate working class and their supporting middle-class college students.

Youth and labor activists formed "6 April Meeting" which became one of the major forces for the anti-Mubarak demonstration on January 25 in Tahir Square in Cairo,Egypt.

In Western Sahara, the Gdeim Izik protest camp was erected by a group of Sahrawis on October 9, 2010. The camp of 20,000 inhabitants was destroyed by Moroccan Security forces that faced strong opposition from young Sahrawi civilians.

Occupy Wall Street settled in Zucotti Park beginning with a festive group of 1,000 people, mostly young folks. Young people are well aware they are part of the 99% and have a right to question the values of the super-rich getting richer. Wall Street still owns the regulators.

The Yale University Occupy chant was "Make change, not money" About 25% of Yale's graduates on graduating, head for Wall Street.   The youth are telling us to reign in the banks, citing the disaster of 2008. Our leaders won't do it because they believe they would be interfering with "financial innovation". The young know better and want to do something about it, and have the guts to do so.

Indigo teachers of the metagifted, Wendy Chapman and Carolyn Flynn, authors of THE COMPLETE IDIOT'S GUIDE TO INDIGO CHILDREN, explains the children are here to demonstrate and contribute quantum intelligence. "They will lift the planet in a hyperspeed way - - being able to understand a situation from a multiplicity of perspectives in an instant. From that, the individual processes the information in seconds to arrive at the most empowering and uplifting outcome. Also vibrant multiplicity -- is the ability to remain vibrantly engaged with multiple projects while maintaining vision and focus for each one."

Parents need to help them cope with their impatience and their giftedness through using what the above authors call a "dialogue compromise:" Help them create their own disciplinary solutions.

When trying to choose clothes for school or making other choices –

"Give me two ideas and we'll decide which works best."

"I love you too much to argue with you about that."

"That might be an option." "What do you think you'll do about your problem?" --gives him power and keeps the dialogue open.

"Here you come from a place of acceptance and respect. Give them empathy for their struggles. See the rightness in it. Give them guidance in accepting what they cannot change. Also give them validation for their effort to adapt despite the flaws in the structure."

Most problems will be solved simply by listening. Dr. Tom Gordon's book, PARENT EFFECTIVENESS TRAINING, offers specifics on active listening with more dialogue on keeping the conversation productive. His book, TEACHER EFFECTIVENESS TRAINING, was nominated for the Nobel Peace Prize three times.

Chapman and Flynn also stress the importance of brain activity: (Pgs. 218-235)—"The prefrontal lobes of Indigo brains are more developed. - - Larger prefrontal brains are active in a higher state of intuitive knowing (ESP, clairvoyance, etc.) These lobes act as 'wings' of the brain opening our minds to more dimensions of experience. In the future more and more of us will activate this portion of our brain."

Whitney Strieber, author of THE SECRET SCHOOL, (lessons learned on spacecraft) testifies the New Children "are taught to operate on a broader multi-dimensional frequency which helps them access information and knowledge not available to others". Her testimony is similar to Chapman's and Flynn's mention above of "higher bandwidth creativity, and hyper-speed thinking". (Visit her on You Tube.)

The following poem is typical of the feelings expressed by the frustrated Indigo Child. Karen, at age 12, bluntly poetizes a poignant need to remain protectively aloof from adult manipulation in order to "see the facts for herself".

I KISS NO ASS

I follow no footsteps because the ones I start to make I end.

And I don't need your sun

Cause I am my own sun.   I can make light for myself, so I can see the light.

I don't need your gentle fingertips because I have my own two hands.

And I have no room for hassles

No time. I don't have any need for it and it doesn't have any need for me.

You can use your army and shield to knock me down,

But my feet are planted to the ground.

You tell me to "kiss ass".

I want to say, "Don't they know I have a mind, too,

I'm not stupid!''

But what I say is "I kiss no ass."

CHAPTER 2

HELP FOR FRUSTRATED AND SUCIDAL CHILDREN

Art therapy becomes a container for rebellion and bitter feelings and would be especially helpful to Indigo Children. They must learn to cope with excessive frustration daily, due to their mission and high expectations as "system busters". This therapy also provides a way to gratify exhibitionistic needs in a constructive or at least tolerable manner. Children are urged to "give their monsters safe paths on which to walk."

The child's increasing ability to express himself in his art becomes for him an objective measure of his expanding ego strength. His spontaneous projections lead him directly to the source of his conflicts.

Pencil, chalk and paper provide a simplified solution for children's release. Paper is patient. As one little girl confided, "I like you because you give me something to do with my hurt and angry feelings and once they are on paper, they no longer push me around."

It is essential to convince the child that her/his emotions and experience, both pleasant and unpleasant are the stuff from which creative art is made. Art therapy and self hypnosis are two effective methods of release and control of involuntary movements.

It is clear that teachers often do not know how to relate to children in opening their minds to inner vision or imagination. They wonder why children dislike school or are so bored with it—with all the rote learning. Children will hear the 3 r's more receptively if an appropriate time is set aside for acknowledging holistic personhood, allowing a time for sharing feelings or writing and painting about them, as Karen did in her poem, "I Kiss No Ass", on Pg. 24.

Seventeen year old Indigo David referred to high school as a "big joke". After attending one year of college he became a dropout and followed his own creative vision. He had been taught from an early age how to protect his creativity. Too many children have their inner light squelched by authoritarian teachers. At age 25 he had formed his computer company that was generating one million dollars a year; by age 35 his company was generating 5 million dollars a year; and by age 45, his company was generating 11 million dollars a year. He had become a success despite the boredom of schooling. Many Indigos want to become entrepreneurs and work for themselves, not someone else. They rebel against a demanding schedule.

The problems of confusion and boredom with school will not go away until the system changes. Peggy's vision took her into beautiful oil paintings that brought her funds to pay for her college education. This happened only after a struggle with alcohol and cocaine.

The question remains, why are young people so bored with school? Too many turn to drugs and end their lives at an early age. A Stanford graduate student who received A's claimed he did not know who he was and rented a plane to jump to his suicide.

How can we help these children with their feelings of intense frustration and in some cases, hopelessness?

CLOSING THE GAP BETWEEN ADULTS AND CHILDREN

Rob Brezsny visualizes "a New Earth where our children will study singing and dancing and meditation and dream work with as much diligence as we devote to math and science. They'll learn to see with their own eyes and think with their own minds and feel with their own hearts, studying those subjects as intently as they do spelling and grammar and social studies."

The rights of our children must include validation of the whole child! We must stop escalating our numbers of "throw away" children. Since the introduction of behavior modification techniques, too many teachers have swung into an about face, insisting their job is limited to teaching only the three R's. Yet they continue to be baffled yearly by continued, and in some cases, very strong resistances to learning by increasing numbers of children. This resistance has increased with the first wave of Indigo children in the 70's.

Parents are also often pained by the lack of warm communication with their young. Going with the grain of our children's realities often means going against the grain of ourselves, in what we have been culturally conditioned to believe.

We are becoming increasingly aware that the "official answers" are no answers at all, as we are forced to painfully acknowledge that we have more incarcerated children than any other nation in the world and an increasing adolescent suicide rate.

Wikepedia Free Encyclopedia reports on the internet the following: an 8% jump in suicides between 2003 and 2007, the largest jump in 15 years; the leading cause of adolescent suicides is mood disorder; lack of parental interest is the major factor. Dislike of school and lack of academic success in school also contribute.

Jose Arguelles clarifies this self-destruction in his TRANSFORMATIVE VISION; he points out that since creative expression is innate to humankind, when we deny ourselves our expressive wisdom, we deny our own humanity.

I felt that preserving my children's creativity was an urgent undertaking. The public schools often unfortunately have a way of squelching this expression.

Recently there has been some good news about teens, which I believe is due to the influence of the increasing arrival of more Star Children radiating a higher vibration and bringing about changes. The Indigo Children are known for their mission of "system busters", and they have had appreciable impact on the schools.

The Centers for Disease Control and Prevention report teen pregnancy is down. " According to a recent study by the National Center for Health Statistics, 39 0f every 1,000 girls ages 15 to 19 gave birth in 2009, a historic low.

"Since 1990. The percentage of high school students who smoke or drink has declined.

"Fewer teenagers drink or drive or ride with drivers who have been drinking. More students report wearing seat belts, and significantly fewer are involved in fatal car crashes.

"Gun-related deaths involving teens have declined. So has the percentage of high school students who fight or carry a weapon."

CHAPTER 3

<u>MIRACULOUS GUIDANCE</u>

Receiving miracles or attracting them is in itself a miraculous mystery that many recipients have undoubtedly pondered with gratitude. This is especially true when one has not sought them but has been fortunate to have them occur just in time to avoid dire consequences. Is this not proof positive that our angels are watching over us, and deserving of our heartfelt gratitude?

Others have demonstrated that praying for miracles is the way to get them. In the movie, LETTERS TO GOD, several children and adults were cured of a variety of cancers due to their steadfast faith.

Especially fascinating to me has been the "golden thread of guidance". Some prefer this description of a "happening" to that of a miracle that keeps us moving towards a special goal or purpose. Friends and family have demonstrated they are often receiving special guidance.

My former husband found himself heading for Los Angeles without understanding why he was making this trip. It was just two weeks later that we met at a party given by his friends for drama students. I had just completed my teaching credentials and had finished a drama class to bolster my confidence for teaching, scheduled to begin in a few weeks. Being in great need of someone to help me with moral support and paper grading, I was grateful for his willingness to help me in any way he could. Within a year we were married. We both truly believe he had to make that trip at that particular time. I had just finished my teacher training and was hoping to get married, and so was he.

Our son David also had a fascinating "golden thread of guidance" for his future life. He had started college but soon realized "this was not for me", being a genius with computers. He had worked for the computer establishment, GOOD GUYS, getting experience in doing some business management. Here he met four cohorts who decided to begin their own company.   He became CEO of the company and by age 45, it was generating 11 million dollars a year. By 2010, his business had increased another 300%.

My first "guided blessing" was meeting with roommate, Lyla Pillsbury, who became a kind of fairy godmother to me. She connected me with a series of future miracles that led me to become a successful teacher and parent. She moved into the same rooming house in which I lived in Milwaukee, Wisconsin. I had recently left my home to see if I could make it on my own. Leaving took enormous courage for a 17-year old, and I was feeling surprisingly insecure at the time. Lyla was the person guided to me to help stabilize my life.

She was the instrument chosen for several miracles that sprang from our friendship. Most awesome was a fish cloud appearing in the sky as a confirmation of and support of my work in teaching children how to release feelings of hurt, fear and resentments. This work was based on Dr. Dorothy Baruch's Teacher Training Group, an event that was made possible only through my connection with Lyla.

Lyla was working with a counselor, Mildred Greene, who knew of Dr. Baruch's work. MIldred knew I was teaching Junior High School and was feeling shaky in my job with teenagers, fully expecting to become one of the high teacher attrition casualties. Thankfully, she referred me to Dorothy's class where I was fortunate to "go to school with the angels", as my Vice-Principal described it.

Little did I imagine that my first psychic experience of seeing a large grey fish cloud in the sky was the greatest event and most important guidance in my life. I was driving on my way to give a talk to teachers and administrators about helping children release negative feelings, so positive feelings could flow in and replace them. This method was based on the miraculous merits of Dr. Dorothy Baruch's NEW WAYS IN DISCIPLINE, which offered insight into our basic Divine nature. It seemed a message of encouragement as I was singing Bob Dylan's "A Hard Rain's Gonna Fall", wondering if teachers and parents could shift gears on time to prevent a destructive future. Humankind had the H-bomb, potentially lethal power plants and man was destroying the biosphere.

The fish symbol looked so large and solid, I thought it might be a new missile from the military. I started to laugh suspecting this might be a special message for me. I rolled down my window to ask the driver in the car next to me what to make of it. At that moment the cloud form whisked away.

After many years of bewilderment over the meaning of this symbol, seen in 1965, the writing of this book in 2011 finally illumined its meaning. This experience redefined my life. It was my introduction to the reality of a personal God. It was the first of several visual communications that deepened my trust and faith in the guidance of a deeply personal God. The fish was the symbol of Jesus' "underground network". He sought to re-establish on earth ethical and spiritual ways of living. When planning a meeting with His disciples, a way of announcing the meeting was to draw this symbol in the sand.

Beneficently, Dorothy Baruch's writings brought new inspiration and hope, emphasizing the release of negative pain and feelings so Divine love and creativity could radiate. She believed this love needed to be shared with one another and that it would eventually bring world peace. "We need to learn to lead by the word and not the whip, as Jesus did," she said.   By God's grace, I was led to become a member of her teacher training group.

This training enabled me to encourage children to share their dreams and many miracles presented in the following pages.

CHAPTER 4

ESSENTIAL REDEFINITION OF HUMAN PERSONALITY

The timeless question hauntingly remains: What is a human being anyway? We yearn to know, is it true that we're using less than 10% of our potential? With the energy of our consciousness, we humans have been documented as being able to bend a spoon, deflect a laser beam, influence an electric magnetic field and cause a photo to appear on film without a camera, change the temperature of water, reshape a light in an object, and make space glow with light. The SUPER PSYCHIC KIDS, demonstrate more awesome abilities on You Tube and in the book, by Dong and Rafill, CHINA'S SUPER PSYCHICS.

SInce the publication and award winning movie of the true case story of SYBIL in 1972, more credence has been given to the concept of multi-dimensional personhood.   Coincidentally, SETH SPEAKS was a parapsychology best seller in 1972 and in 1983.   It, along with SYBIL explains this bewildering phenomena in compassionate and powerful terms, with reincarnation portrayed as more than plausible theory. The human personality is illustrated as consisting of various levels of intelligence and creativity, each yearning to express through some channel. Helpful and aware adults can assist the young in making choices as to what inclinations, talents or abilities will manifest for the purpose of creating a life filled with meaningful learning and consciousness expansion opportunities.

Past life experiences appear to influence these inclinations or choices, or how else does one explain children's early giftedness manifesting without previous training? At age four, daughter Suzanne announced herself as an artist. She picked an iris and did a crayola sketch of it complete with buds. Her artistic expression later developed in a mature artistry and a prosperous website. She sold her glass paintings for $600 to $1000. Mozart's MINUET FOR PIANOFORTE was published when he was just five years old; Einstein's biographers tell us he did not begin to speak before age three, and when he did, he spoke in math models.

A willingness to learn from children's spontaneity has supplied the key motivation for this book because children consistently reveal their wisdom if we are willing to tune in and truly hear them. The "New Children" have arrived to teach us transcendence to a new level in evolution. Most important for children and adults alike, is the ability to responsibly create one's "personal reality" through energized thoughts, emotions and imagination. It is important for the adults at this time, to be led by the children. Many spiritual leaders have repeatedly illustrated the primary lesson of Jesus to "love ye one another", as we put forth best efforts to also create a harmonious consensus reality. Broader creativity frameworks are essential with the leadership of these children.

Limited personal and global perspectives urgently need refining and clarification. As Chief Seattle suggested in 1951. "All things are connected. What befalls the earth befalls the sons of the earth." It is crucial at this time of ecological imbalance that humankind once again acknowledge its human and divine aspects and strive mightily to restore balance and harmony within, so this may extend to our beloved EARTH. We must stop projecting our frustrations and destructiveness onto one another and onto the environment, as such blindness can only result in a death culture.   Many authors believe the Star Children are being born to help prevent such an occurrence.

Many persons are discovering a deeper intra-psychic relationship with different levels of themselves, and as they reassimilate their personalities, they begin opening up to and perceiving a rich storehouse of solutions to current challenges and problems. In your personal life be alert to stories that tend to provide evidence for the fact that all of creation is conspiring to give us exactly what we need, exactly when we need it.

One of the unique gifts available to us at this time is Quantum Jumping, a program composed by Burt Goldman. We are put in touch with other dimensions of ourselves for whatever our needs may be. Good health, improved relationships, money, achieving goals, success, abundance, becoming a better writer, musician, painter, photographer, overcoming fear, and whatever other emotional needs we may have. He is helping us discover the infinite universal wisdom , success, health and creativity that is awaiting us. What a boon this is for the Star Children, many of whom are painfully bored with the public school curriculum.

Burt Goldman has an extensive background in collecting wisdom from around the world. He has studied qi or energy and the control of this energy in Korea.   In Hawaii, he studied with a Kahuna Master; Kahunas believe we are multidimensional beings and live on many different levels of the self at the same time . Later Burt learned the art of meditation from Paramahansa Yogananda and went on to explore hypnotism.   He then became proficient in hand acupressure and began healing and teaching people to heal by simply pressing on two parts of the subject's body with the middle fingers of his left and right hands. Healings occurred in minutes, and sometimes, seconds, he notes. When he heard about Jose Silva's mind control seminars he became his number one instructor for the seminars. He later studied the Chinese Art of Feng Shui, became a Psychic Healer and mastered Neuro-Linguistic Programming (NLP).

Wendy H. Chapman, Author of THE COMPLETE IDIOT'S GUIDE TO INDIGO CHILDREN, is one of the few brilliant pioneers responding to the needs of the Star Children. The many parents of Star Children that have been complaining that the schools have not been helping their children develop psychic and intuitive skills, now breathe a sigh of relief.

Her curriculum includes advancing children's intuition, imagination and 6th sense. She teaches metaphysics with children in developing creative visualization skills through guided imagery and takes them on Imaginary Field Trips. She helps them develop meditation skills and psychic talents such as: Intuition Classes (increase your mind to receive clarity and direction re. one's inner voice and 6th sense); Sacred Geometry; Crystal Use and Healing; Shamballa Healing Classes (Wendy is a Shamballa Master Therapist); Shamballa Reiki   for Children (a method of healing energy that works on all levels including the physical); Quan Yin Healing and earth healing .

This is only a partial list. It is encouraging to read her entire resume on the internet. She has graduated Magna Cum Laude from the Univ. of Connecticut and has an M.A.in Educational Psychology.

Zak Martin is referred to as Britain's leading psychic. He has established his own consultancy at Kensington, London. His clients include royalty, politicians, pop stars and heads of major companies.

He was a musical prodigy and could play every instrument without musical training. His book, HOW TO DEVELOP YOUR ESP, details extrasensory perception in all its forms, including telepathy, clairvoyance, precognition, and psychometry. He emphasizes, "As your psychic abilities improve, so will your powers of creative self-expression - - in other words, your musical and artistic abilities will be considerably enhanced as your suprasensory powers come to the fore."

There is a New Age desire to explore the greater reaches of human consciousness, to realize and appreciate that individual creativity is now being demonstrated as originating from various levels of "minds within" and is playfully, humorously, cleverly expanding and redefining itself through action. Each in time discovers the SELF to be a unique personality gestalt network unto itself, joyously responsible for his/her uniqueness and creative contributions. This network includes great compassionate assistance from one's oversoul and in turn, is connected with a vast, universal creativity.

The nature of this very personal and private bond with aspects or spirit helpers manifests itself in celebration and independence of organizational structures that, perhaps unwittingly, seek to control or repress the individual's creative heritage. Discovery of one's unique "personality gestalt:" brings an enormous celebration of resurfacing psychism and the discovery of our human heritage estate as co-creators of the universe. We now are enabled to create a more enlightened and harmonious reality, born of a comprehensiveness that includes global as well as personal realities, embracing all species upon the earth, not exclusively the family of mankind.

Increasingly, many of us are discovering we are, and have always been psychic, but most of our cultural foundations and religions have demanded repression of these ancient expressions and abilities in order to control and impose restrictive rules and behaviors, for various "advantages". It is time to enlighten this repression and guarded impotence that cannot now explain nor substantially resolve personal-social-global snarls of varying magnitudes, by comprehensively reconnecting with our wiser, stabilizing teachers within.

If one can accept the Seth concepts that there are no accidents, no victims and no coincidences, and our SNARLS in these areas are clearly meant to evolve questions that will lead to satisfactory, congruent problem solving.   Many individuals are discovering that changing one's personal or global world does indeed depend on changing one's belief structures, which crucially includes getting in touch with one's hidden beliefs.

To assist with this process, increasing numbers of individuals are experiencing "inner hearing" or what has often been referred to as "spirit guides" presenting direction for resolving personal and social problems. The Quakers have been demonstrating this process for centuries and have much good company today, as Marilyn Ferguson's "sunshine drenched" pages of AQUARIAN CONSPIRACY disclose. Ferguson elucidates this change as a "A great shuddering, irrevocable shift . . . overtaking us. . . . It is a new mind, a turnabout in consciousness in critical numbers of individuals, a network powerful enough to bring about radical change in our culture." She seemed to be aware of the large wave of Indigo children that had arrived in the 70's at the time she wrote her book in 1980..

World renowned psychotherapist , Carl Rogers, also stated at a conference that he felt " good about and with psychic phenomena," perceived as helpful forces and energies offering new hope to a crumbling culture: "I am one of those who see our western culture as having reached its culmination , as now approaching its death, and hopefully, its rebirth into something new and strange to us. I'm far from being alone in such a perception." He seemed to have a premonition of these new children so advanced in intuition and psychic abilities who would soon be teaching us how to develop and use these for our improvement.

For too long, Church and State have ignored or denied or not understood the individual divinity and the creative potential needs of the people. In so doing, the great power and harvest of individual growth with its creative contributions and solutions has been greatly suppressed or lost. During our current whirlwind transition, many are joyously coming to a fuller recognition and appreciation of who they are and what they can do. They will now be led beyond their present state of fear, depression and powerlessness. The "New Children" are here to help humanity ascend to a higher vibrational frequency that will enable us to live out our life's purpose, and discover the gifts and talents we have to offer.

CHAPTER 5

AN OPEN, HONEST FORUM ON GLOBAL PROBLEMS

In 1983 it was disclosed that many teachers were unable to bring themselves to discuss the TV film "The Day After", which was presented as a consciousness raising effort by the ABC network. As a result, UCLA at Santa Barbara offered a seminar to help persons cope with this "unspeakable fear". A local group of counselors are also offering a course in "Education for Social and Political Responsibility" to help individuals find the courage, love and support to speak openly of the challenges of personal pain and violations; of exploding global populations; of our disappearing rain forests with the consequences of changing climates; the poisoning of our air, water and soil; our rising coastal waters resulting from the "greenhouse effect", and of the crucial controls needed for our nuclear power and resulting hazardous wastes.

Non-violence is an increasingly sought goal among thinkers reflecting on the possibility of nuclear holocaust. The public schools have made Martin Luther King's birthday a holiday to honor his heroic efforts in reaching and demonstrating his dream of non-violence. It appears that any change in society must include a comprehensive look at what or who is doing the violating, and it is obvious that each of the above global issues is life-threatening, or clearly in violation of humanity. Many young people feel an increasing state of fear and powerlessness in adults by the lack of openness on these issues.

Overpopulation has played a key role in all the aforementioned problems and challenges. Many articles have been written about the "population curse" in China, India and Mexico City. The latter is a demonstration of a hellish nightmare, due to the governments ban on abortions and meager contraceptive knowledge. Only in the case of rape is abortion allowed. It is a frightening example of the crushing threats of "killer smog, shocking sanitation and rampant corruption". At this present time, Russia, China and India are the worst polluters.

Too few teachers are willing to present the facts and connections between global population explosion and global instability, and yet this is the primary challenge to our young. The fear and lack of open discussion on these issues is the same silence, fear and distrust of each other that is tearing family life apart, driving many to drugs and drinking. It is time for us to be truly open and learn from one another, brainstorming with everyone possible, so effective solutions may have an opportunity to be heard.

Rob Brezsny brings good news to lessen the fear of children and adults, noting that things are getting much better on earth. "The world has become dramatically less violent since the end of the Cold War, and we are now living in the most peaceful erasthe human race has ever known. - - - Death rates from cancer are declining; - - - In 2006, UNICEF reported that the death rate among children had declined dramatically since 1960. Back then, 184 of every 1,000 kids expired before age 5. More recently the number is 72 per 1,000.

"Nobel prize winning economist, Gary Becker, reported that between 1960 and 2000, life expectancy in the poorest nations on the planet increased from 41 to 64 years. Economist Steve Radelet reported one of the most crucial shifts in human history began around 1980. After rising steadily since the beginning of time, the number of people living in absolute poverty has fallen by nearly one-third in less than three decades.

"A further reason for the sharp reduction in child mortality has been improved medical treatments. These include immunizations against measles, rehydration therapy to combat diarrhea, Vitamin A supplementation, and the widespread use of bed nets to foil mosquitoes bearing malaria. Measles has been one of the most virulent diseases in Africa and Asia. But since the Measles Initiative to provide mass vaccinations, the death rate from measles has dropped 74 percent globally and 89 percent in Africa. Thanks to widespread vaccination, two other success stories stand out; the final defeat of smallpox in 1977 and the looming victory over polio, which is very close to completion. United States foreign assistance programs helped save millions of lives over the last several decades.

"The rising rates of intermarriage are helping to dissipate ethnic and religious strife worldwide; Americans' IQ's have been steadily rising for a long time; the number of people living in poverty in the developing nations is declining dramatically; the world is becoming more free and is now the most free it has ever been; the acreage devoted to organic farming is increasing rapidly all over the world; we cheer forest protection activist Odigha's successful campaign to preserve the last remaining rain forests; most HMO executives now believe prayer and meditation can expedite the healing process; that vast supplies of frozen gas lie beneath the oceans, harboring more potential energy than all of the world's oil reserves and could be mined with the right technology; the giant timber company Congolaise industrille des Bois, voluntarily agree to stop cutting down trees in a virgin forest in the Congo.
"An impossible dream was fulfilled when the world's largest private bank, Citigroup, agreed to stop financing projects that damage

sensitive ecosystems. It promised to invest more in projects that use renewable energy and to pursue projects that protect indigenous people.

"In the future, shrinking oil reserves and global warming may impose limitations on your ability to use cars and planes and other machines to travel. But you also know how many smart and idealistic people are diligently striving to develop alternative fuels."

Now we have the Global Summit that delivers a whole system approach to address humanities many initial challenges from the ground up.   We must put our trust and efforts in the communication and problem solving abilities of humankind, instead of withdrawing in fear. Fearful withdrawal and denial means the surrender of personal creative power to a suicidal course. High level denial efforts will not banish the problems we have created for our resolution, nor will it ease the pain of increasing alienation experienced by so many, because no discussion forum is available. Only active communication and action will help us back to an understanding and blessing of the ONENESS between all creatures.

This kind of holistic approach says to the child that what you say and experience is important. Your contribution is important. You, as a human being, are to be HEARD, UNDERSTOOD AND NURTURED. Our nation is in deep trouble because too many people feel unimportant and afraid. We must find our way back to a communication that celebrates the ONENESS between all humankind and all species, and restore meaningful purpose to our lives. There is more compassion in the world now than ever before.

We need to change our belief structures and accept a redefinition of human personality so all nations may benefit from its enormous creative potential. We also need to reverse the destructive trend of pushing too many of our young into a depressed state of powerlessness.

At the present time the creative voice of our young people, tightly programmed into twelve years of school, is seldom   heard in all the daily rush to "stay on task" with the 3 R's.   Instead, the rush invalidates the holistic child and often weakens self esteem.

As the flower yearns to burst forth to experience the sun, rain and the process of flowering – with the flower giving way for the seed to experience renewal – so do children yearn to express, flower and flourish in their "time". They yearn to "flame forth" their inner potential.

Children are creatures of creative expansion, seeking ways and opportunities to express inner talents and abilities, just as their parents and teachers are. They are not "objects" to be manipulated as mere grist for the educational mill, or for any other system. While behavior modification brings control benefits in cases of extreme disorder, it also places restrictive conformity demands upon the talents of too many others. The individual must alter behavior, mood and attitude which serves to inhibit or suppress creative contributions.

Feelings of powerlessness and frustration in our teachers bequeath the same anguish to our young. Too often teachers have not been encouraged to pursue the creative arts or to brainstorm for creative solutions to blockages within. Some educators believe that humans are not born good – that they are not filled with a God potential that enables them to be unlimited powerhouses for the creative good, -- but rather they must safely conform to restrictive curriculum frameworks for their own good. The "New Children" have arrived to change all these misconceptions, as they lead humanity to higher vibrational awareness.

CHAPTER 6

<u>CREATIVITY NEEDS MUST BE MET AND CONSTANTLY ENCOURAGED</u>

Carolyn Kenny suggests that rigidity, getting stuck or the inability to deal with a new situation . . . lack of adaptability, fear of the unknown are all concerns of the disabled and of mankind as a whole. At this historical time the "New Children" are here to shift our consciousness to help us change. They will teach us to make better use of our abilities and help us to further develop our psychism. As we ascend to our higher source we will learn to live out our life's purpose and discover the talents and gifts we have to offer. These children will teach us how we can best counteract rigidity, decline and further social disintegration by revitalizing a healthy respect for the creative inner spirits of one another.

Carl Jung insists that everyone has a drive to be creative which must be satisfied. This drive can create products beneficial both to the individual and to society IF the proper channels are discovered. He warns that if the creative instinct is not used or properly channeled, it can have a harmful effect on both, the individual and society.

THEY ALL WANT TO WRITE has been a popular text for teachers of creative writing in elementary school and the title holds the key to the needed nurturing of the creative spirit of our young people. Caring adults can help them make an early commitment to creativity and spare them the pain of feeling their lives have been without purpose or meaning.

Kenny refers to a medical monopoly that further seduces and disqualifies people from fighting the good fight in politically struggling for a healthier world. These are individuals disconnected from inner creativity who are angered, sickened, and impaired by BOTH their industrial labor and leisure. By forming the habit of consulting the doctor or psychiatrist, they had come to believe they can escape ONLY into a life under medical supervision.

Studs Terckel's WORKING is a play that portrays each "worker's" job leading into another's with the unifying themes of powerlessness and frustration. Many of these are prime candidates for the medical monopoly because they've never learned how to direct and actualize their inner potential. It is powerfully analogous to what takes place in many classrooms which become reciprocal circles of frustration and denial. The educational needs of the "New Children" are forcing this old pattern to change.

The fearful suffocating pattern of fearful authoritarianism – 'We will do it my way, and/or, we will deny it my way, because I am wiser, stronger, older, etc." comes from teachers who do not even keep up with world events because they find it "too depressing". This uninformed "authority" must yield to an enlightened acknowledgment of the ONENESS between us all and to the recognition that we have the creative power to solve our problems. We must come together in this effort.

Carl Rogers, psychotherapist, also notes that our schools tend to turn out conformists and stereotypes rather than truly creative and original thinkers. We must identify what is wrong and move beyond sterile stances, sterile exchanges and sterile relationships that result in sterile successes and accomplishments. Instead we need emotional education that can free us of fear and anger, so we can become informed and dedicated stewards creatively restoring in the ecobalance of our planet EARTH.

We have been long overdue for a paradigm shift in earthly probabilities, but thankfully the "New Children" are here to force us to take an open, honest look at the existent problems and concomitant release of the enormous creative problem solving energies bottled up within individuals. Our institutions have kept too many of us painfully unaware of our unique and powerful abilities which translates into fear and doubt of individual divinity and creative potential. We must realize that individuals are born good and yearn to actualize that drive into effective ideals.

We have been going through a rip-off process and we must end it now. Denial and dummy time will finally give way to recognizing and rejoicing in the full understanding and expression of human personhood. To discover the "meaning of becoming" is the essential creative purpose that can assure personal and global sanity and survival. The question rises hauntingly and repeatedly: to what end are we putting in our time and energy in raising our children? How responsible is our environmental involvement? Will they be ready and able to fight the good fight? Liberty demands constant alertness and response.

Time and what we do with it is the most precious thing we have. By viewing ourselves and each other as multidimensional resources for creative solutions, we will be able to meet the "rapid-change" challenges of this decade. We shall redress the overwhelming probabilities that threaten ominously and appear hopeless at first glance.

As long as people remain alert to the violations of personhood which must include the many forms of pollution caused by overpopulation, ozone depletion, climate change, desertification (loss of land due to erosion and climate change) deforestation -- loss of rain forests, ocean dead zones, species extinction, shortage of fresh water resources, acid rain,-- and continue to discuss and act on them, there is no HOPE of redress.

Rob Brezsny, author of PRONOIA, offers a hopeful perception of our future. "We know clearly what's happening to us, we have all the world's knowledge available at our fingertips, and some of our best and brightest are working hard to come up with solutions. Many smart and idealistic people are diligently striving to protect the environment through alternative fuels, etc. We cheer forest protection activist Odigha's successful campaign to preserve Nigeria's last remaining rain forests."

Each of us needs to strengthen our faith and belief in ourselves. We will then be able to strengthen our ability to take action and trust that others will do likewise.   When people feel they have a measure of control, they feel less fearful.

We will come to discover that what fortifies and sustains us in time of tragedy or disaster are those inner inclinations we have been willing to take the time to heed and develop. Kenny identified a special personal protection and tranquility bestowed in working GENTLY with one's inner creativity; in focusing on positive creativity, -- depressing or violent scenes that try to impinge on one's reality are dismissed. We also discover a restorative magic in this process as we experience that nothing is more effective in recharging one's batteries. This also brings the "peace that surpasseth understanding".

Third grade Tina prophetically summed up the task of the safe global futurist, when asked about her favorite wish."I wish I could know God," she said thoughtfully.

"And what does that mean to you, Gina?' I cautiously asked.

"Know what the people need", was her startling and wise reply.

If we have no concern for honest inquiry as to what the people of the planet truly need, we may indeed perish from tolerating too many sterile exchanges in communicating with one another. We need to accept our responsibility and respond to it from all levels of our personality, in trusting to the vast creative wisdom of the human soul. The time has come for the "New Children" to lead us in this endeavor.

CHAPTER 7

<u>CREATIVE RELATIONSHIPS EMANATE MAGIC AND ENHANCE PURPOSE</u>

I vividly encountered the Issue of teacher burnout when I created an opportunity to go on tour with a variety of central California schools as a substitute teacher. It seemed that everyone was suffering from various degrees of powerlessness in our culture and a lack of understanding as to recovery. I believed that if I could understand firsthand the belief structures of individuals that caused them to surrender power to beliefs of unworthiness and pain which led them to experience needless fear and even panic, I would understand how we all manage to create our oppressive personal and classroom demons and self-defeating behavior. In answering these questions raised by my observations, I hoped to acquire the wisdom and skill necessary to identify and permanently avoid these same pitfalls. This understanding demanded extraordinary alertness, as we are a society heavily conditioned by artificial guilts and shoulds, so that denial of responsibility for selfhood and personal vision remains the biggest fly in our ointment.

As Psychologist Wayne Dyer states in THE SKY IS THE LIMIT, his experiences and studies disclosed that the most persistent barrier to self actualization is the authoritarianism which he finds so rampant in today's society. Many teachers and authors agree with him.   Some teachers who perceive teaching as a nurturing profession are courageously struggling to undo this unfortunate conditioning by heroic efforts to improve communication skills. They offer as a necessary first step the avoidance of making students feel "wrong, bad or stupid" by refusing to listen to them, but to attune to them on various levels – telepathically, as well as verbally, emotionally, and through body language.

These teachers, along with Indigo teachers Wendy Chapman and Carolyn Flynn, support students in their efforts to communicate fully. Indigo teachers Wendy Chapman and Carolyn Flynn of the metagifted have suggested examples of "compromise dialogue" on page 19 of this book, that helps children, especially Indigos, to cope with their impatience and giftedness. Authoritarian "tunneled vision" is thus avoided through encouraging more openness and discussion. These teachers assist colleagues as well as students by asking confronting, exploratory questions:

What are you doing? What is happening now, in our conversing? – uptightness, anger, frustration?

What succeeds?

What doesn't work?

What do you need to do or give up to achieve our goal?

This line of questioning offers assistance to others to stay on purpose and to make creative choices towards this end.

Questions that lend insight and assistance to maintaining creative relationships include:

What's happening?

What are you getting out of this relationship or this way of relating?

Is this the way you really want to be?

Some teachers, afraid of themselves and their responsibility to inner direction take comfort in hiding behind outmoded symbols and shoulds. They attempt to impose their rigidity, fear and tunneled views upon others, by stifling questions along with the benefit of discussion. As teachers are increasingly becoming aware today, The "New Children" will no longer tolerate this fear and rigidity.

I had become convinced ten years ago, when working with disturbed children, in a clinical setting, that the best dispeller of powerlessness was individual choice of joyous creativity. Rejoicing through the discovery of creative power was possible not only through the arts, but through simpler expressions of exercise, gardening, loving communications with pets or plants or improving "p.r." with one's neighbors.

The power of personal choice as primary rejuvenator was unforgettably illustrated through the case of Freddie, an 11-year old boy who suffered with involuntary movements, as reported in Margaret Naumberg's studies of free art expression in disturbed children.

Recently a TV Newscast from Los Angeles reported this syndrome to be on the increase and showed a roomful of young people caught in the anguish of involuntary movements. Naumberg had observed that only through creative design of his choice was Freddie able to procure total relief.

His struggle to be in full charge of his personality and abilities elucidates the pain suffered by many young people today. They are too often discouraged or cut off from discovering their multi-dimensional personhood of talents and abilities. They want to know how to direct their "real power" of mental and emotional focus into free choice priorities that will clarify and strengthen their abilities. Verbal sharing or reporting, reading and writing can and should revolve around concepts that fascinate them. Teachers of creative writing are well aware of this highly motivating power key.

Many children and students report school experiences as dull, irrelevant and even degrading. Little or no effort is made to educe inner abilities by helping them stay in closer touch with their real feelings and honest inclinations. Their revolution in terms of mental and emotional unhappiness uncomfortably parallels Freddie's desperate physical message.

Accidents, drinking and drug abuse are at an all time high, with teacher burnout on the increase. I find myself fascinated with the recurring question: HOW have we managed to do this to each other? Manipulations for power or power tripping are due to feelings of powerlessness or unworthiness. All want and need to express the heroics of inner power. All want to actualize ideals and contribute to personal harmony and a better world. Clearly each needs to be in close touch with inner direction in order to discover that "YOU ARE THE MAGIC", and can face and resolve personal challenges and opportunities. What could be more interesting and fascinating than discovery of selfhood?

A rejuvenating vision of clarity, direction and purpose in the education of our youth is being demanded by all participants through a variety of revolutionary upheavals and needless suffering. The Indigo Children have been applying their "system busters" mission to education. They want to see big changes in education that now lag far behind their expectations. As usual, the young are demanding it more than the teachers who often presume to have the "power over" youth. Youth increasingly demands that their adult world now act as though they were capable of understanding that they have the power to influence, but never the "power over".

A safe environment that supports youth in experiencing themselves as powerful and responsible is crucial to optimum development not only for self, but for all of society. It seems that youth is fighting for its soul against inane curriculum demands, a brainwashing process that fears its full flowering, and too many oppressive adults out of touch with themselves. Creative relating with each other provides a powerful support system for growth and discovery of purpose. As many teachers are becoming aware, the curriculum must now provide new understandings and challenges for minds and abilities of the much advanced "New Children".

Unless love and respect for self and others is foremost in the classroom, a willingness to hear, understand and support each other cannot take place. One of the most enjoyable and immediate connectors with young people, I discovered was a viewpoint from the Palomares human development program.   In a particularly disruptive 6th grade, I made the statement that "Every feeling and statement of yours counts, whether you think it's silly or not." One girl confided, "I wish our teacher would say that. Are you coming back tomorrow?"

I am not suggesting dispensing with the three R's nor the removal of firm limits and boundaries that are clearly understood as essential to optimum classroom development. But many hassles can be eliminated and cooperation freely given by youngsters who know their feelings and inner potential are key priorities in that development. Resistance to essential curriculum learnings disappear as if by magic, and the teacher comes to realize that repetitive dull drills are no longer needed. More time is available for the more interesting, exciting discovery of personhood.

What is personhood anyway and how does one discover "purpose" are frequently asked questions. Knowing one's self or discovering true identity is an unfolding process that consists in acting, speaking and writing ourselves as we go along. In other words, we come to know who we are by what we say and do. It may change from hour to hour, month to month or year to year. It is dependent upon an inner multi-dimensional richness of talents and abilities and the individual's choices as to what shall manifest. It hinges upon a willingness to consistently attune to inner impulses, nudges and directions. More children are coming to know their life's primary purpose by the time they reach the 8th grade, expressing it through consistent, strong interests or impulses. The "New Children" are here to help these personhood discoveries occur even earlier.

The beneficent impulse can be distorted if a child cannot stay in close touch with self because close touch with feeling has been discouraged, as, for instance, telling boys not to cry. OUT OF TOUCH means OUT OF CONTROL. So a first concern must be with emotional education in encouraging the release and redirection of the powerful emotional energy behind hurt, anger, fear and anxiety.

Eckhart Tolle, author of THE POWER OF NOW, believes that one of the first things that will be taught to first grade children in school is to watch and indentify their feelings in order to instantly change them. Children need to "become aware not only of the emotional pain but also of the 'one who observes,' the silent watcher." This is the power of the Now, the power of their own conscious presence.

For example, one evening when I was playing the piano, someone knocked on my door. I felt anger rising, because I did not want to be disturbed. But in identifying the anger instantly, I could change it to calmness and not let it control me.

There are two primary concerns with discovering and experiencing identity or personhood. Identifying and releasing powerlessness feelings of anger and fear is one, and replacing those feelings with newly energized ideals, wishes, or aspirations is the second. Redirecting energy into the latter is a key issue.

The "New Children" are famous for their abilities to heal and to even change DNA. (See pg. 15 of this book) They are also teaching others to develop these skills or to experience vibrational cures so that hopefully within a few years these present sad problems will seem like ancient history.

At the present time, the power of self-healing is urgently sought by children suffering from leukemia, cancer and other illnesses at Dr. Gerald Jampolsky's Center for Attitudinal Healing, in Tiburon, CA. Again, the all-essential step in physical and emotional healing is to release fear and anger.

The children made a list of "Things You Can Do About Your Feelings" and the importance of finding the courage to share them together. "We found it helpful to find other kids who have similar problems and to meet with them...You can choose to help yourself by speaking up...Don't fight your angry feelings. Just accept them...It's ok not to cry...to be mad that this is happening to you."

"Before we got sick, we didn't use words like 'hope' and didn't talk about God very much...We thought our parents could make anything bad go away…Before we got sick we didn't feel helpless but after we got sick, we did."

They drew pictures releasing their fears of seemingly endless blood tests, of shots, pain and hair loss from chemotherapy and teasing from other children, making it clear that one has a choice in all these matters. For example: "When other kids tease you, you can pay no attention to them; you can fight them; or you can choose to see that they are scared. (We found that sometimes kids tease you because they are the ones who are scared.)"

Some drew pictures aggressively directing their energies into having the white cells beat up or destroy the black cancer cells, in an effort to increase the white blood cell count. One child drew a personal angel of hope slaying his personal demon of illness.

Forgiveness and learning to use the NOW point of power greatly aided healing., " Forgiveness to us meant not blaming anyone for anything…"letting go of the past" (not hanging onto it) and forgiving everyone and everything sure helped a lot in not being so afraid. We learned to say, NOW is the only time there is."

The most wonderful choice of all was that "We found we could decide to be happy inside even though we didn't like what was happening to us on the outside."

When Dr. Jampolsky and these children went on the Donahue Show addressing the needs of children coping with and fighting cancer, it won an Emmy Award. It was a revelation to many to hear several of the children candidly claim that, "Because I have assumed responsibility for my illness, I have a chance to reverse or arrest it." They were attesting to the discovery of their great self-healing energy power and sharing it with many skeptical others.

In Dr. Jampolsky's RAINBOW book, the children stated how helpful it was "to find out how other kids looked at death." One child shared, "When you die, your body leaves you and your soul goes to heaven. There it joins other souls and becomes one soul. And sometimes the soul comes back to earth and acts as a guardian angel to someone." The children agreed, "We all seemed to like that way of looking at death." I also include descriptions of some drawings by children at a New York Summer Camp because of their valuable instructive symbolism. The children were described by psychologists as withdrawn, disturbed or retarded, but were clearly releasing highly charged messages of symbols from within which led to self understanding and healing.

TOMMY AGE 5, AUTISTIC

Tommy drew a picture of himself and his psychiatrist father, who expresses himself, in Tommy's opinion, quite well – with arms protruding from the head. Tommy has neither arms, legs nor ears in the presence of his father which may indicate he feels his mind could be suppressed or overwhelmed by the father.

In the next picture Tommy draws orange arms, legs and ears on himself (when not in the presence of his father). Orange is frequently symbolic of happiness and knowledge, and it is of interest that Tommy has also framed his picture in orange. Perhaps he feels that in time he will be able to express himself and will do so knowledgeably.

ELLEN, AGE 9, RETARDED

Ellen has drawn what appears to be a figure similar to a box kite anchored to a very tiny house, surrounded by flowers in the midst of which Ellen is playing and thinking her own happy, childish thoughts. She has drawn three patterns directly above her head. As the house is representative of the environment or of the child herself, the message might be that Ellen is aware she has such expansive thoughts that it is impossible to fit this awareness into so small a body (house), so she has just parked it temporarily until she feels she will be ready for it. In the meantime, she is enjoying the happy, childish thoughts of a six year old (or retarded child).

TONY, AGE 6, EMOTIONALLY DISTURBED

Tony has drawn a lopsided house (or environment) and he appears to be leading an adult (possibly representative of the adult world) because he wants to show people everything is crooked and the message here seems to be, "There's got to be a better way!" To the far left of the picture, there are two birds, symbolic of the mind flying free, the smaller one again leading the way, showing the bigger bird.

Tony's thoughts are similar to those of the Indigo children who have come as the "systems busters" because so many things "are crooked", and they are eager to teach us a better way.

FRAN, AGE 9, RETARDED

Fran has cheerfully drawn herself and some flowers representative of the simple thoughts of childhood. She also has shaded her face with grey, indicating she may feel restrained and would like to break out of what is restraining her. The orange ball flying towards the sun seems to indicate that this is what she would really like to do, i.e., aim for the highest. The yellow insides or "tummy", scribbled over again with a restraining grey, may portray the message, here is a child who feels very bright and would like to break out of whatever is restraining her.

It is generally accepted that what most distinguishes man from the lower animals is his ability to symbolize and to communicate to others by way of symbols. An attempt to classify and describe various symbols along with a precise manner of studying symbolization both in normal children and those with psychopathology has been presented by scientists " who bring their knowledge and disciplined thinking to bear on a field that has, unfortunately, of late received little or no scientific attention." (Royce, et al, 1965).   One may speculate as to the origin of these insightful messages out of the mouths of babes. Increasingly, the children encourage all to heed the messages of wise and powerful teachers within.

Elisabeth Kubler-Ross, M.D., has done extensive research into life after death. She shares her observations that "it is impossible to die alone" and presents dying as a "butterfly in process of leaving the cocoon." She affirms that "When we are slowly preparing for death, as is often the case of children who have cancer, prior to death, as many of these children begin to be aware that they have the ability to leave their physical body and have what we call an out-of-body-experience (OOBE). All of us have these OOBE's during certain states of sleep. Very few of us are consciously aware of it. Dying children especially, who are much more tuned in, become much more spiritual than healthy children of the same age. They become aware of these short trips out of their physical body which help them in transition, -- which help them familiarize themselves with the place to which they are in process of going. It is during these trips with dying patients, (young and old) experience, that they become aware of the presence of beings who surround them, who guide them and help them.

"Young children often refer to them as playmates, the church calls them guardian angels, most researches would call them guides. It is not important what label we give them, but it is important that we know—that every single being from the moment of birth, which begins with the taking of the first breath until the moment we make the transition and end this physical existence – that we are in the presence of these guides or guardian angels who will wait for us and help us in the transition from life to life after death."

What import do these "loving beings" surrounding children have on the role of classroom teachers? I believe it has strong implications for helping children and students discover purpose and create high quality lives for themselves. It is also obvious that the curriculum be restructured and flexible to accommodate the "new children" with their gifts of higher abilities. They will, of course, be teaching us how to do this, as their purpose is to teach us how to ascend to a higher vibration in thought and feeling.

Redirecting energy into positive goals, such as self healing, is a process called co-creating which becomes clarified with the child's enjoyment of a more harmonious reality manifesting according to individual ideals or wishes. Certainly within the classroom a child can experience personal choices and joyous growth to an appreciable degree when the home environment denies such opportunity. Choice is always the primary motivation, and in order for the child to feel more aliveness is that he or she really counts, it must be experienced.

Returning again to the primary concern with emotional education, the Seth literature clarifies that one intense emotion has more than enough energy to send a rocket to the moon, which is illustrated through the demonstration of children participating in healing themselves of catastrophic illness.

Some of my most powerfully instructive experiences came from kindergarten and first grade children demonstrating their creative power and beauty daily through art, poetry and one-liners. We had an open, sharing environment focused on emotional education in which the children were encouraged at least three times weekly, (20 minutes per day approximately) to release hurt, anger and fear by drawing about it, acting it out with puppets, fighting it out with family dolls or sandbox battle scenes, or painting about it.

After this pent-up release, the loving aspects of the child fairly glowed with magical inventiveness and presented in paintings that were brighter and better organized, in new lotto games, puppetry dialogue, new skills, more energy for friendships and courage to "fight the good fight" or assert self as needed. Resistances to learning faded.

Not only could they see and hear what was going on around them with greater clarity, but they were able to attune to and direct personal positive expressions with a power and grace that was poignantly moving. It was possible to glimpse their "inner blueprints" or abilities which surfaced strongly in many instances.

I never doubted that I was fully in the presence of God whenever this impulse or blueprint sharing occurred, and I was grateful to be able to pass on these fine techniques developed by Baruch and Axline to my two children. David and Suzanne have grown up sensitive to their artistic and mental gifts, with the ability to actualize and express themselves most effectively.

Bringing forth these results was dependent on setting boundaries wherein the children felt safe, allowing negative awareness of hurt, fear and anger to surface, to be owned and safely released. Their present and past life demons of oppression or suppression were given "safe pathways on which to walk", and their more positive, joyous expression waited just beneath the "release", eager to be heard in all its loveliness and power.

Proof positive of the effectiveness of this method was offered to me by the Principal of Belvedere School in Tiburon, California, where I was teaching a 6th grade class: "I don't know what you're doing with this group, but keep it up. They have not been willing to cooperate in the past, but always seemed to go off on separate tangents. And their achievement test scores have improved remarkably."

The miracle I could never fully identify in this process is one that appears also to have eluded Dr. Dorothy Baruch. It seems that participants may have inadvertently put the child in touch with powerful belief structures from reincarnational past lives as well as the present circumstances of parenting.

In giving full and loving acceptance to the present personality, no matter what had been said or done in the past, in terms of authoring gods or demons (e.g., actualizing ideals or reinforcing fears) great positive energies were released. The self image was strengthened, freeing spontaneity and creativity from past bondage.

Dr. Tom Gordon notes in TEACHER EFFECTIVENESS TRAINING the importance of active listening as it "promotes a closer, more meaningful relationship between a teacher and a student. Students who are heard by their teachers invariably experience a sense of greater self-worth and importance. The satisfaction of being understood, coupled with this increased self-esteem, causes students to feel warmly toward the teacher who listens. The teacher feels a similar warmth and closeness. - - - Listening empathically , walking a few steps with a student on his life journey, is an act of caring, respect and love. This is why we say teaching can be a form of loving."

When the repressed energy charges of several lifetimes is released, belief structure about self image and others are given an opportunity to change, and the positive comes surging forth exuberantly as guilt trips and outrage drop away. The channel to power is more effectively cleared.

This "miracle working" method included the magic ingredient of focusing on the child only and listening with every ounce of tenderness one could muster, with full acceptance of the child's feelings. In this way, caring was demonstrated through setting aside "time alone" and offering the reflective listening or mirroring dialogue which led to new compassion and understandings. This process resulted in a restructuring of relationships for all participants.

The greatest gift we can give other human beings is this gift of complete understanding and compassion. We let another know that no matter what has been said or done, mistakes can be understood and learned from, energy can be redirected, that one is indeed acceptable and cherishable just because one IS a human being.

Maxwell Maltz stresses in a positive image builder that you are NOT a mistake, because the Creator doesn't make mistakes. He points out that while we may make a mistake, our mind can get in control by correcting course. But there is a great difference between being a mistake, and MAKING one. When a person is once "programmed" as a mistake , by being called stupid or through subtler forms of undermining, then he will find it difficult if not impossible to believe in his corrective power, or to take action to correct his course or direction, and to realize the kind of life for which he longs. In utilizing Dr. Baruch's approach, we need to help another person see that s/he has the freedom to choose to get in better control and management of himself and his circumstances.

In this way we haven't missed our opportunity to safely guide the child's expression of releasing feelings. If s/he guiltily hesitates or attempts to disguise anger at a parent, we need to help the child with active target identification. It is often frightening for a child to own up to anger felt towards the two most important people in one's life, when one is so dependent on their love and support. Much reassurance is needed In a first "release of feelings " experience.

The child then comes to see and believe there are safe adults in his world who will be fair and greatly encouraging of his inner spontaneity and giftedness. In this manner belief structures from past lives may be powerfully shifted, which allow a reorganization and redirection of energy into positive outcomes.

1. Feeling Identification: (hurt, anger, fear, etc.)   "Looks like you're feeling pretty mad at Suzy for grabbing away your truck and toys."
2. Person or Object Identification- - - In this instance, the person is 2 ½ year old Suzy. When the target is not so clear, it helps to say: " Feeling angry? Don't know why? That's natural. Lots of people get angry without knowing why."
3. Channel Identification- - - Stop the hurtful act at once and provide a safe "channel release for the negative feelings, as it is impossible to STOP feelings. "I can't let you hit Suzy or push her off the playhouse as you seem to want to, but you can take your feelings out on the tether ball, or tell me about it here. Later in time alone, you may take your feelings out in the clay or draw or paint about them if you wish!"

As one child confided, "I like you because you tell me what to do with my feelings so they don't push me around any more."

Firm limits also need to be set: 1) You may not get too loud or too wild; 2) You may not do anything hurtful to yourself or to anyone else; 3) Reassure the child by universalizing, Everyone gets hurt or angry or afraid sometime. I do and dad does. This is a good, safe way to get the feelings out where we can't hurt ourselves or anyone else.

This method is highly effective from age two on. Children saw at once that the adult was most importantly a listener to feelings and that understanding and directing power of emotions was all important. This compassionate listening in "time alone" for 15 or 20 minutes, at least three times a week reconstructed the relationship into one where the child felt safe, loved and understood. The safety of natural grace feelings provided new courage which was greatly enhanced with total acceptance of the child as good, no matter what he or she had said, felt or done. Limits to behavior were set and definite non-violence values stressed quite simply in the statement: "You may not hurt yourself or anyone else."

Honest sharing of feelings about events in the classroom or on the playground teaches values and deepens love and trust of self and others. Acknowledging, validating and supporting each other's expressions and feelings, and demonstrating a willingness to hear one another enormously strengthens everyone's self image. Violations of each other can be powerful illustrations of non-love and non-trust of self. The child or adolescent will also transfer and apply these learnings to home and neighborhood.

From the alpha state one can also enter into a family member's physical and emotional state, thus eliminating second guessing in understanding and determining compassionate response. This exercise, entitled "Putting On Heads" is detailed in the POWER OF ALPHA THINKING. Dr. Baruch emphasized the necessity of tuning into and understanding the child's feelings "with every ounce of tenderness you can muster", and the same attitude applies to telepathically interfering.

Now it is possible to more fully comprehend the mental-emotional state of a child or mate who may be physically ill or emotionally upset, and communicate comfort and healing, while receiving invaluable feedback that builds compassion and understanding, thus strengthening the bonds of love. A change in belief systems may also be initiated.

Adult consistency, playing together, winning cooperation and firm limit setting of boundaries through natural consequences of actions and family councils were also highly effective, as offered by Dreikurs in CHILDREN THE CHALLENGE. Encouraging adults in class to bring fuller, freer expression while clarifying one's boundaries for optimum spontaneity, autonomy and non-intrusiveness was strikingly similar to the release and process used in Dr. Baruch's "time alone" with younger children, of owning feelings and channel release. In the NATURE OF PERSONAL REALITY, Seth also suggests adults beat a pillow to achieve the latter.

Closely allied with this state of safety or natural grace is joyous exuberance, often described as playfulness. It also affirms a gut level conviction when Seth assures us that we have never lost our state of natural grace, no matter who may try to control or convince us by attempts to engender artificial guilts or fears.

We are part of ALL THAT IS or GOD and our right to exquisitely exist , whether expressing clearly o r "lost in mazes", is part of this vast, all encompassing heritage. Seth's compassionate insistence that "even those mazes are creative"- - - emphasizes the need to aspire towards fuller comprehension, eliminating intolerance and judgmentalism. Total acceptance of ourselves as good and in a state of grace is the foundation step for co-creating. The SELF then acts spontaneously as a unit, adjusting automatically with different levels (inner/outer voices). This occurs only when the conscious mind has not accepted conflicting beliefs so a sorting out process may be required fist.

Thoughtful response to the child's feelings then allows the child to perceive the belief structures underlying them, and to change those beliefs. Ongoing at home "releases" are hitting a punching bag or beating a pillow, and dream programming to settle conflict in the dream state . (See lucid dreaming, Ch. 10, Pg. 96/97 and Dream Exercises, Pg. 114)

First and foremost is the belief that there are safe, caring adults who actually care about so vital a force of the soul's expression, namely the intelligent directing of emotional energy. Resistance to learning the 3 R's disappears as a stronger, cooperative bond unfolds, and joyous creativity surfaces. The relationship is dramatically restructured into one of mutual trust, cooperation and loving communication, which takes from about two days to two weeks depending on participants.

In terms of creating reality, we can see that coping with the enormous release of power in anger, fear and its concomitant involvement with developing sexuality , calls for methods and approaches enabling the steering of these great energies into joyous, loving, constructive expression which is the epitome of spirituality. Spirituality is a concept often distorted into surrendering power to other systems or hiding behind another's symbols instead of accepting responsibility for recognizing, facing and replacing anger and fear. One can then use this newly released energy to actualize ideals.

Instead of seeing the facts for oneself and directing one's emotional energies, many believe it is far safer and much more comfortable to project their guilt and discomfort onto undeserving others. The natural consequences of such denial or hidden beliefs results in further suffering through illnesses, accidents or ruptured relationships.

I am convinced that if a teacher operated from the framework that every child can be reached because s/he was born good, this is precisely what will eventually occur. The practicality of relating with one's peers, teachers and classroom activities also requires emphasis. One of my best learning experiences was with a hard core disturbed group of 11-year old boys in an unusual school district that valued awareness and innovation, and was open to new learnings from, and experiments with disturbed children. Recognition that one is born good includes appreciating and affirming the body as good, since the body is a manifestation of the soul in flesh. What one thinks of self – physically, emotionally, mentally and spiritually, determines behavior and "altogetherness" or the lack of it.

Ron is an example of a child out of touch with his unrecognized and misdirected energies of fear and anger, regarding sexuality, that exploded into violence repeatedly. I met with his special education class consisting of eight boys each week, and for about twenty minutes took the most violent boys for a "time alone" session for identifying and releasing feelings in order to change the underlying belief structures propelling their destructive behavior.

Clay is usually the child's chosen media for expressing feelings. So we began with my urging them to create any symbol that represents any feelings of hurt, anger or fear, including hurtful persons in the clay. They were helped to understand that most persons have these feelings and it is wise to face them and get rid of them for clearer sense of purpose, and for understanding and improving relationships. After making a clay model or drawing or writing to express their feelings of pain from which they wished to be free, they were asked if they would like to talk about it.   The teacher used "active listening" skills as described in Dr. Tom Gordon's TEACHER EFFECTIVENESS TRAINING. Some responses were to smash the clay, chop it, or throw it in the fire. One boy made a speeding car that possessed power over everything in its path.

This scene gave way to giggles and the rolling out of clay penises that they began to throw at each other.   I tried to mirror or reflect back to them what was happening: "It looks like you have uneasy feelings about your bodies and growing up, and you need to know especially that the Creator made every part of you good. Do you want to tell me why you feel this is something to giggle about or why the penis is not very important. Because this is what you are saying in throwing the clay around, and that must stop right now or we will have to stop   this session."

With these boys where violence was rampant in their daily lives, limits had to be firmly insisted upon. Sometimes the best way to show love is to stand firm in the face of chaos or mayhem. This stance has been referred to as "tough love".

Again I emphasized, "Every bit of you is good. Every bit of your body from head to toe is good and beautiful." They laughed a good deal at first, and then I said, "You can draw anything you want to about your bodies and express the fear or uneasiness which is coming through as giggles. The giggles are usually a cover-up for uneasiness."

One boy confided, "My dad hits me so hard, I think its going to fall off." And then he drew a big penis, furiously exclaiming, "O, fuck this and fuck that." Then followed an erupting volcano and he seemed to be releasing much pent up violence. I reassured him with, "That's great that you can get all that anger and disgust out. But you have also got to love yourself real good—every bit of you—from head to toe. The penis is also the important part of your body with which you can help create babies when you're grownup."

Later, at recess, when these boys were outside playing, Ron picked up a rock and threw it at his friend, cutting his face and narrowly missing his eye. Immediately he fell to his knees and sobbed over this violence which was "par" for his day as a rule. This was the first time anyone had ever seen him moved to compassion. He had never been known to cry and this spontaneous behavior signaled a breakthrough in new perception and understanding.

Another first grader described as "soft core disturbed" included Marty who at first drew a battle scene fantasy of a cowboy surrounded by Indians. This appeared to be his way to at first avoid direct confrontation with his anxiety. "Here's Daniel Boone shooting the Indians and I'm Daniel Boone," he explained. I mirrored back his feelings: "It looks like you're afraid of these Indians." He shook his head yes. Then he turned the over the paper and drew a picture of 12 missiles explaining, "I am a giant in control of the missiles.'' Next he reached for another paper and drew a large picture of himself with a penis which he at first described as a "giant with a penis." When I asked him who it was, he said quickly as he scribbled over the penis, "It's nobody." I reassured him the penis was a good part of him, as the

Creator does not make mistakes, and he needed to love himself really well.

Opposite the giant he happily sketched a house with a large Christmas tree and toys, and a smiling Monty waking up Christmas morning full of expectation and joy. This release produced a creative breakthrough in him that afternoon. When for the first time in first grade, he went to the art table and made a large two foot accordion pleated Santa to take home. He had never ventured into any creative artistic expression since he entered school until this day. With the creation of the new Santa, he seemed to be saying, "Because I am good and fine and feel good about myself, I can trust Santa to love me and be good to me. It feels good and safe to make my first artistic expression at this Christmas time in this way."

Many children yearn to know in similar fashion that their bodies are good and they have a right to good feelings about themselves, instead of being imprisoned or immobilized by artificial guilt and fear. Hard core or soft core disturbed are now mainstreamed into most classes, with teachers needing new and viable frameworks and strategies for effective teaching.

The same issue kept recurring as to how well teachers understood their deeper responsibility in providing opportunities for creative exploration of value fulfillment, so the young might truly get to know themselves. This deprivation was aptly expressed in a gifted high school senior's musical lyrics and composition which he shared with me along with his general feelings of frustration and boredom, despite his "A" grades.

His lyrics spoke straight to the anguished grip of powerlessness, indicating how teachers "help us keep our fears" by laying their same old trips and tapes, and lamented how all of us seem to overlook the divine miracles within ourselves. He encourages a forward look into one's inclinations or talents and a steadfast refusal to keep the mind in "chains of fear" as so many of his teachers were obviously doing to themselves.

Fortunately, the Indigo "system busters" are creating a close look at what has prevailed and they are initiating immediate change in several school districts. The system busting is taking hold, but moving slower than the frustrated Indigo Children hoped for.

I was particularly sympathetic, remembering how my son refused to don the traditional cap and gown like a proper graduating senior, because high school was "just a big joke". Fortunately four caring teachers and an interest in tennis and math kept him from becoming a dropout. He accepted an honors award that paid his tuition through a computer training institute, much relieved to be free and well on his way to mental and economic freedom.

Because he responsibly actualized his inner impulses, today he thoroughly enjoys his accomplishments achieved through the release of his inner talents. He acknowledges his achievement as his own, despite the numerous frustrating obstacles placed in his way by high school personnel, and their efforts to take credit for his success. He learned to strongly stand forth and say, "This is mine!" – particularly when the military began to harass him for his talents, due to the cooperation of high school personnel. His success in forming his own computer company, becoming President and CEO with 80 employees happily acknowledging him as a "people person" and their delight in working for his company, was a blessed outcome for his energies and talents.

Youth will ultimately win in compelling change within the institution of education because many more parents are sufficiently aware in directing their children to be strongly autonomous and spontaneous, true to their inner direction. The Indigo Children have also come to help in demonstrating this change.

Terman's Stanford University follow up studies of the gifted disclosed several who knew themselves and their primary interest or "life purpose" by age 14. Mozart, Haydn and Einstein are also examples of early discovery, revealing their primary life's purpose in musicianship and mathematics. But with many more parents today making the effort to help children clear their "channel to power" of hurt, fear and anger while attuning to inner direction or impulses, early discovery is increasingly widespread.

Many of the Star Children know what their purpose is. They have come with a new vibration to transform the consciousness of humanity. The Indigos are here to topple old systems that lack integrity: the government, environment, legal, educational , health care systems and much of society. They are clearing the path for the Crystal Children who are arriving to demonstrate peace and love in all their actions, living the "Law of One" or global oneness.

It was a joyful time to observe my children "announce" their purpose at an early age. My daughter, Suzi, announced herself as an artist at age 4 by picking up a tall iris, laying it on the sidewalk, and then sketching a remarkable resemblance in yellow, orange and green crayola, complete with buds and leaves.

In high school, my son David found himself so enthralled with the possibilities of computers, that he would often forget to eat lunch. Some high school boys, including David, had been encouraged in an experimental computer program at the nearby college. When the computers, had to be moved one rainy day to a nearby town, David hopped the bus in downpouring rain to follow and continue his research. "Greater love hath no kid," I chuckled, and his primary interest continues to be computer design, programming and inter-facing. He has become a millionaire because of his persistent interest and now has a website detailing the services offered by his company.

Many individuals like to explore several roles, however, and surprise themselves with newly emerging talents at a late age, such as Grandma Moses, the artist. History may record her primary purpose in life as an artist, even though from her perception, the motherhood role may have been every bit as important. However, luxuriating in one's abilities and risk taking are also essential to unfolding personhood and purpose.

Creating more exciting and promising probabilities demands risk taking. Young people are also now presenting evidence of having experienced a quickening of their intuitive and insightful abilities. Many are adept at reading a teacher's aura, intent and motivation, and are able to sort out the hollow manipulators from the truly caring, safe adults. Most of all they are learning to appreciate and work with powerful inner forces of multidimensional talents surging into their awareness, despite classroom oppression because they treasure knowing themselves above and beyond the external signals of grades, pleasing the teacher, or getting trapped in systems of reward and punishment.

Many children have suffered persecution in varying degrees from the adults in their lives for their participation in this quest to know self. The marvel is that they managed to maintain an inner/outer balance, regardless of what was done to them. It is essential that we experience the multidimensional fullness of our own personalities in order to feel fully alive and growing. This attunement to our inner selves has been celebrated in several songs, such as the Muppet Movie Song and "The Rainbow Connection", which asks children if they remember being half asleep and hearing voices telling them what they're supposed to be.

In the following pages, guidelines for adults in affirming and protecting the child's creative power, allowing s/he to sort out personal beliefs and those of the culture, hopefully will contribute to eliminating the violating of personhood that many children now experience. Crippling blows are often unwittingly dealt the young from adult "innocence", lack of awareness or authoritarianism.

The fear of powerlessness or surrendering power to fear is also being expressed by teachers as well as youth.   Many seem to feel a deprivation in understanding the inner needs of self and one another. These include self sufficiency, inner stability and tranquility, unique expression of creativity in activities and relationships, as well as opportunities to rejoice in the beauty, pleasure, power and harmony of one's personal reality which each "choicefully " can create. As one girl remarked, "It's crucial to find what you love to do and do it!" And such joyous personal accomplishment always benefits others.

As Dr. Wayne Dyer suggests, when one is deprived of these needs, s/he becomes "just as sick as if deprived of adequate nutriment." He urges, "Don't die with your music in you!" Anxiety, depression and illness are usually the result of not having these needs met. Their fulfillment was and is dependent on consulting inner signals or impulses consistently.

A Junior High School teacher was the first to express his concern for teacher survival and confided over lunch one day: "I know the kids are angry but what about my feelings in this daily battleground? There is the constant fear of losing control. Usually there is just one or two who can turn a class against me."

Another teacher expressed concern with burnout indicating that many were resigning each year despite a high unemployment rate and tight job market. "Frankly," he advised, "there are not many caring teachers. They just seek to survive. They have to. Those who care will suffer the results of the non-caring influence and sink with the rest of them. It won't be long now."

A Senior High School teacher disclosed that three handguns had been taken from students involved with gang warfare the week I visited this school. A kind of run-away fear was clear in the faces and voices of these teachers. Most concluded that more "authoritarian moxie" was the answer, without efforts to motivate rebels to get their best, constructive selves "outfront". Creative motivation is essential along with setting "tough love" limits, or the boundaries and limits are not respected.

After a shared semester of experiences and grievances, it became increasingly clear that the top priority in saving ourselves as educators had to be new awareness of beliefs and nurturing for ourselves – if we are not merely to survive, but strengthen selfhood and remain effective, beneficent classroom influences. An awareness of support systems and joyousness triggers or playful activities is as important to survival as the techniques, methods and knowledge in teacher training.

At a specially called "survivalist" meeting, one teacher proposed making a list of the persons and events that gave us maximum strokes for time and energy invested, and to turn to these often. This type of support system enhances the self love and self trust that are key to nurturing and stabilizing growth. One needs to see through and also learn from personal games and hidden beliefs to strengthen this love and trust.

Resistance to making the commitment to creativity can be clarified through getting clear with one's priority goals or purpose, and then asking often what is needed for commitment of completion. In considering goals, some second grade children in Caroline Schneider's second grade realized they would need to give up feeling stupid, worrying, working too slow and feeling "I can't". Their reminders are helpful to looking at our own blockages. (Sometimes at the piano, I feel too inept to master the next arrangement and put off any serious effort to do so for days. I have noticed that identifying the feelings around resistance helps to quickly dispel it!)

We were looking for ways to support ourselves in new, creative ventures. We wanted to know and experience ourselves as fully as possible, so we could share this process with children. We recognized that teaching is a framework or learning opportunity that we set up for ourselves. It raises many questions and encourages much creative problem solving, all for our beneficent enlightenment and growth. We were also encouraged to write love letter to ourselves by way of reviewing and appreciating our beneficial characteristics, abilities and accomplishments. We could clearly see how important self love is to the ability to love others and that we needed to achieve an appreciation and understanding of non-violation towards self if we were not to continue blindly violating others.

Along with the love letters, we recorded lists of anger and guilt, with the surprising discovery that much of the latter revealed itself as artificial guilt. Needless worry and suffering is created by taking on the tapes of someone else's projections, particularly in the area of guilt.

After these exercises, we realized that all desire value fulfillment within a framework that is not punitive but embraces artful living through fulfilling spiritual and biological yearnings. The acknowledgement of ourselves as being born good and able to express as unlimited powerhouses of creativity, no matter how discouraging family background or present family conditioning might be, is an essential first step to creating the reality desired. Unfortunately, many teachers at the present time cannot accept this framework.

But unless they are able to set examples and self actualize goals or ideals themselves, how can they hope to demonstrate faith in self of new awareness to others? This expansion process calls for flexibility, a non-dogmatic stance, joyous optimism and a joyful willingness to learn with and from the young. Empathy, sympathy and outgoingness are vital to this on-going development.

A willingness to acknowledge our historical time as one of transition of paradigm shifts or sudden changes in all areas of life seems crucial. This flexibility helps in the avoidance of anxiety and fear and provides the keen awareness necessary to shaping viable classroom curriculum.

A flexible curriculum permits educators to at least keep pace with the youth who have learned how to face their fluctuations of creativity, and provide the space that will encourage them to experience and express what they yearn for above all, namely their expression of inner creative power, and problem solving in light of the very challenging world they have inherited. Rob Breszny brings a positive global report to lessen everyone's fears. (See Pg. 37 and 38)

Most important are the underlying belief structures of the teacher that enable her/him to meet the challenge of   the rebel in each youngster expressing the pressure and pain of powerlessness. These students often perceive no caring acknowledgement of their uniqueness

– no interest in or support as a result of the widespread practice of herding young people together and treating them all alike.

The worst example I encountered of this practice occurred in a combination 3d-4th grade that also contained one third emotionally handicapped children. All were assigned the same pages from a 4th grade text. Many movies were ordered and used as tranquillizers. There appeared no opportunity to express inner creativity at any time. This teacher expressed himself in a near-hysterical manner, talking rapidly, perspiring , and totally changing his lesson plan on film and filmstrips at the last minute. He repeatedly stressed how good the kids were but he talked so fast, it was nearly impossible to understand him. I was stunned into bewilderment as to what unidentified fear and guilt were driving him, creating his exhausting, hyperactive behavior.

Truly caring teachers are always inspiring to encounter. I was delighted to meet Caroline Schneider, author of, I KNOW YOU LOVE ME, taking a large group of children through some jazz exercises in the auditorium early one morning. What most impressed me was her gentle yet firm way of communicating with these little people. Even the most withdrawn child was able to de-ice and enjoy participating in her rhythms class.

It clearly centered around her concerns and caring about them. She quickly won the cooperation, laughter and trust of this group by picking up a little girl and requesting her to feel electricity through the tips of her fingers and toes – and to freeze like a statue as she turned her upside down.

Later she told me that those who could not participate in the reading or math programs because of withdrawal, would find themselves easily involved with rhythms and music. It was rewarding to see them so happily involved. Her flexibility and creativity allowed her to meet their needs to express and enjoy life at school at least for a short time.

A wise person once said, "In education, if you can't give them anything else, at least give them rhythms and music." I think this statement suggests keeping children attuned to the enjoyment of life by giving them joyous, life-affirming ways to express.

In her book, Caroline presents an outstanding example of children supporting and learning from a behavior problem child to change behaviors as a peer group: "Two years ago Mark Smith came into my second grade classroom. He could not stay in his seat longer than two minutes. Every time he walked by other students he poked them. He could not concentrate on his work and talked like a three year old. On the playground he threw rocks and always said it was someone else's fault. While he was in first grade, his teacher decided that Mark was out of control, could not cope with school and should therefore take the drug, retalin.

"On the first day of school, I called Mrs. Smith to ask if she would be willing to have Mark stop taking the drug, so that I might work with Mark more directly and not through the retalin. She was hesitant, but did agree to talk with the doctor. I, too, talked with the doctor. Both agreed to having Mark come to school without taking the drug.

"The first couple of months were rough, and yet it was exciting to work with Mark directly. One of the first things I noticed immediately was how the students began to lock Mark into his patterns. They would laugh when he talked like a baby. When anything was missing, they would immediately suspect him. They began to call him stupid and make fun of him. On the playground other students called him retarded, teased him and goaded him into breaking rules and then came running to tattle on him when he did.

"Gradually, all of my students began to realize that Mark was no different than they. With their growing awareness and my assistance, they began to notice their own patterns and behaviors. They began to see that he, like they, had his own particular barriers to handle. As a result, rather than locking him further into his patterns, they began to shift as a group to support him in handling his barriers and letting go of his patterns. When he said something cute and babyish, they didn't laugh. When he did something they didn't like, they dealt with him directly, rather than tattling to me. One student requested to sit next to Mark to help his with his work. Whenever he accomplished anything, they acknowledged him. As Mark's mirror, they, along with me, began to allow Mark to see he always was a person with all behaviors and abilities who wanted to be accepted and who wanted to succeed.

"Every month the children in each class at school chose a student to be Citizen of the Month, and that student was recognized before a school assembly. In the spring the children in my class chose Mark.

"After the voting I looked at Mark and said, 'You did it, Mark. You kept at it and did it all. Congratulations.'

"When I began to speak to the rest of the class of seven and eight year olds, I began to cry. In spite of my tears and wavering voice, I managed to say, 'I want all of you to know that there was no way that Mark could have done what he did, without your love and support. Thank you.'

"WE MUST BE WILLING TO MEET OUR CHILDREN AND STUDENTS NEWLY EACH DAY. I realize what I'm suggesting is not easy. It means we have to be continually aware of how we make decisions about our little people and our young people. It means we have to continually asking ourselves daily, Have I made a decision about this young person, and am I establishing a belief system that no matter what the cost, has to be right?

"We all have judgment within us. We wouldn't be complete if we didn't. The point is to not allow our judgment to be the filter through which we see our children and students. Until we are willing to become aware of our judgment, and until we are willing to notice how we tend to pigeonhole and label our children and students, there is no way we can have total and complete communication with them. When we realize there is no need to fear our judgment of them, then, and only then, can natural communication exist between us."

The violence expressed at the early childhood level reflects the confused beliefs and behavior of many adults attempting to nurture without understanding that we are a culture now in transition, just like the rest of the planet.

There appears to be an accelerating force within each consciousness striving towards fuller expansion and expression that requires the acknowledgement and support of caring adults. The utmost in flexibility and resources is required to effectively communicate and help at this time. Without a knowledge of the "ground rules", or of what is occurring, one can indeed feel knocked flat or trampled at the outset!

The lack of self love and respect, confusion and violence of preschoolers , kindergartners and first grades was often expressed through foul language, throwing sand or clay at each other, fist fights, and general bedlam. Punches and pinches were occasionally inflicted on the teacher and teacher aids. Children sometimes had to be forcibly restrained.

"How did all this come about and how much worse can it get? " was the question in the minds of teachers I talked with. The priority question was always the same. What kind of belief structures create this particular classroom reality or gestalt? How do we transcend it?

We need to recognize that it is a matter of trust and belief in limited or unlimited free choice that we got as far as we are, and in this way we can begin to glimpse how our "safe universe" works. If we are oppressive and hurtful to self or others, natural consequences are forthcoming. Respect for self and others is always foremost in co-creating.

We are clearly at a time in our history when "the saints are coming through". Aside from the arrival of the "New Children", lovingly strengthening our intuitive and psychic abilities, inner/outer calling cards are also plentifully present. More children are experiencing psychic phenomena externally, as well as the accelerating of their internal psychic abilities. Recently, 12-year old Laurie, a daughter of a class friend was awakened by her radio suddenly switching on and the appearance of three mysterious, round-shaped lights in her room. When she turned the radio off, it came back on. This occurred three times and was somewhat frightening. Laurie is a quiet, almost shy child who is very fond of animals and an intense lover of nature. This "calling card" seems destined to keep her asking questions. It is, by its somewhat startling nature, designed to do so.

One mother wanted to know how to explain such an experience to her child, and her neighbor shared her carefully meditated answer. "Just say this could be a communication from another dimension of yourself and it's beautiful and means your growth. But remember, you are the one in control here, and this is a chief responsibility. You must decide how much contact with other dimensional visits. Tiredness must not occur. You must rest when tired so that any illusion of negative take-over cannot develop. High, positive energy is needed for positive experiencing. You have a hand in creating ALL that happens to you."

More children are learning to perceive auras and enjoy reading their teacher's mood of the day or moment. My daughter, Suzi, at age 11 enjoyed this new perception, and recalls a most outstanding aura of lilac and gold emanating from her High School art teacher. It was particularly brilliant when the woman bent over to pick up some pottery, as it flared up powerfully from her neck and back. "This is the best, brightest one I've ever seen, mom," she enthused. She was also stunned by her science teacher's lovely emerald-green aura that just seemed to be there unexpectedly one afternoon. He, as well as the art teacher, had demonstrated a special empathy and love towards the students.

Clark Moustakas, psychotherapist , in LONELINESS AND LOVE, tells of a supposedly withdrawn third-grader, Bill, who was defined as a non-reader and non-learner by his teacher. He had communicated only in monosyllables and was defined as "oddball and retarded", necessitating the inquiries of a psychotherapist, who was fortunately empathetic. The therapist describes himself as being intrigued with Bill's attention span and his sustained way of pursuing questions. He also disclosed a "giftedness" in chemistry, biology, electronics and magic. His inner reality included a keen interest in ESP, out-of-body travel, poltergeist phenomena, precognition and clairvoyance. He had used the technical terms appropriately and related them to his own life. "I have to control my thoughts," he said, "because if I let them go, strange, mysterious things begin to happen. When I concentrate hard, I see spirits in the furniture, ceiling and walls, and once our table moved without anyone touching it."

The " New Children" have come to help lead our weary world into new hopes and understandings.   Dr. Gerald Jampolsky's collection of children's insights and drawings in CHILDREN AS TEACHERS OF PEACE, also offers refreshing, prescriptive advice.

Ernest, age 12, urges the world to increase its capacity for loving: "When you and your country love your children more, there will be peace forever."

Joelle, age 12, suggests that "Peace is helping someone live, live happy, live strong,. Sharing. Sharing your feelings, your love. Sharing life with the world deep inside yourself.''

"Peace is talking. Talking aloud words of wisdom, words of love, words of life. Talking within one's self, of love, of feelings. . . Peace is friendship. The trust, the accomplishing feeling."

Gloria, age 10, advises, "Never put anyone else down. Because everyone makes mistakes. And I would also say always get along with other people."

Sandra, age 11, urges caution and continuing patience with the difficult: "There are those that you can't get along with even though you've tried hard. Try to avoid them at first and then slowly start saying more and more nice things to them. It might work. This method could start with a few individuals and soon nations could begin saying it to others and become worldwide. It could become a nicer world."

Jack, age 12, shares a poignant glimpse of the pain felt by families torn apart by war: "To the leaders of a country, a few more casualties in a war is nothing. But to the families of these people, war has taken away a part of their hearts and lives. Leaders should realize that being imperialistic is not worth one family's suffering."

Sarah, age 10, shares the wisdom that killing others is like killing part of ourselves:

"Life is like a seed, a flower seed.

A flower seed that is planted.   Life goes on and the flower seed starts to bud.

It buds a pretty little flower bud, a nice life.

If you treat life like life, the Flower will bud and bloom.

But when you go to war you crush that Flower

And its life is gone just like yours.

Let there be no war and let your life go on

And let that Flower grow and bloom.

 How can you let that Flower grow and let your life go on?

I know peace."

Haley, age 8, extends a special invitation to reflect on the meaning of peace: "Peace is the sun that gives us light and keeps us warm. Peace is the moon that glows and shows and keeps us out of fright. In the night, every little thing that grows and shows how much it cares.   It's the meadows soft, green grass; the animals out of danger; waterfalls flowing and you know that the world is safe. NO war! NO killing the animals or anything, a bed of daisies 100 miles each way; a sweet smell in the air; butterflies and buttercups of wondrous colors; trees spreading seeds all over the ground and all you hear is the trees blowing; the wings of the butterfly. Of course, this is only my idea. Why don't you write yours?"

Christine, age 12, reminds us that we have a "very best" self that is much needed: "Peace is when people do not fight. There is no prejudice. And all people join as one, each person their very best self."

Finally, Susanna, age 10, urges us to turn within to solve our problems of conflict. "Peace is when you have a soul. . . when you have a friend inside to be grateful for."

With the arrival of the "New Children", listening to one's inner voice is on the increase for all age groups and in all walks of life. Dr. Jampolsky refers often to receiving advice in this manner. In his tape recordings and books he refers to "miracles" occurring in his work because of his willingness to heed the advice of his inner voice. He uses the definition of a miracle given to him by Dr. Bill Thetford as the following: "A miracle is a shift in perception that removes the blocks to the awareness of love's presence."

It seems our planet would benefit greatly by listening and learning from the experiences of children. It has been an urgent concern of some parents and teachers that unless teachers give children maximum opportunities to express this inner vision, all are losers; children and adults have been suffering the deprivation of sharing in one another's talents and abilities. However, The "New Children" have come to change these concerns, by demonstrating they will be heard!

Children also now seem to be more open to their inner voices or teachers because they have not been subjected to societal conditioning that largely demands denial of this phenomenon. They are, as a result, often able to teach the world with clearer vision. The "New Children" are leading the way in this major transition.

CHAPTER 8

AVOID SUFFERING WITH A PARADIGM SHIFT OF INSIGHTS

Just as heeding one's inner voice can open doors to a wide range of creative approaches and solutions to daily problems, so can the oppression of tunneled vision lead to fear and tragedy. Many persons yielding to the oppression of fearfully limited choice are into gloom, doom and many kinds of destruction –- often in the name of being Christian or following Jesus.

A recent illustration was the attempted firing and maligning of the good name of an elementary school custodian by a family brainwashed with cult techniques that demanded the surrender of feeling and thinking for self to fearfully organized and oppressive symbolic dogma.

A kind of frenzied "protection "against self inflicted devils is sought by cult advocates because of a need to erect barriers against their feared inner signals. Consequently they suffer much fear and guilt. This frenzied guilt is then projected onto others. The case of Diane, in HOLY TERROR, by Conway and Seigelman, dramatizes this invalidating, dehumanizing process, which was applied to the custodian who was trusted and loved by those who knew him well.

The two accusing sixth grade girls sought to recover, in their confused way, from deep feelings of boredom and powerlessness. They wished to demonstrate a distorted form of their power. It was negatively expressed as "power over" this adult who had befriended them many times. But he had attempted to limit their exploring the boys' bathroom, and they accused him of sexually molesting them. It carried overtones of the Salem witch hunt all over again; this time it fortunately miscarried. Those who knew personally of the man's good character and family life were able to persuade the jury to acquit him. However, the ugliness of the trial has seeded doubt throughout the community so that pain for all participants continues.

The key issue remains the cry for help from these young people seeking for a healthy expression of inner power. Long repressed from expressing feelings and concerns honestly, by their brainwashed, frightened family members, these girls sought to experience their power much as the 15-year old in Arthur Miller's CRUCIBLE did in accusing Salem women of "evil" witchcraft and conspiracy with the devil. The "power payoff" came in securing the execution of these innocent women much as these sixth graders sought to ruin the custodian's good name and livelihood in this community.

Refusing responsibility for expressing one's personal inner vision into positive, loving reality and opting instead for powerlessness through a preoccupation with evil and devil symbols is not only sad and wasteful visualizing, but the intensely felt discomfort and guilt is invariably projected onto undeserving others.

Real power, as understood and portrayed through the life of Howard Hughes, once the wealthiest man in the world, is of keen interest to students in classes I've visited.   We usually manage to discuss him because it gives us a chance to look at his values regarding wealth and relationships, along with his frightened delusions that led to his emotionally isolated, lonely life and despondent death. Most poignant were his exaggerated fear of germs and his need to don white gloves for "protection".   Poisoning by other humans whom he perceived as objects to exploit and manipulate was greatly feared.

We demonstrate our concept of "real power" according to how we direct our energies. This is intimately tied in with what we value or believe and how intensely we feel. For example, we may become enslaved to a disliked job by opting for the bigger house or car and find ourselves serving empty, non-fulfilling goals.   We must always self-consciously ask: What do I love? What do I hate?

This awareness is crucial to understanding how our emotional energy then becomes translated into our ruling gods and demons, which ripples outward, affecting all our surroundings.

Recently, a talk show interviewed evangelist Oral Roberts and incisively discussed the "messianic stance" of individuals who attempt to impose their values and morality on others, and then insist, "If you don't agree with me, you are doing the devil's work; and with Jesus on my side, I can justify doing anything !"

The leader of the Love cult near Seattle manipulates and controls his "followers" by insisting he is the personal representative of Jesus Christ. He attempts to get his wishes carried out by asking, "You don't think Jesus Christ would let me get out of line, do you?" On a recent TV interview, a former woman member angrily objected, "Using people in the name of Jesus Christ is about as evil as you can get."

Similar stances have been taken by a Joe McCarthy, a J. Edgar Hoover, a Jim Jones or even a school teacher, just shifting the authority symbols around a bit, altering meaning and intensity. The degree to which each of us might be involved in getting others to surrender power to us was also questioned and explored.

I was astonished by the manipulations of a fifth grade boy in a special education class who reportedly suffered from feelings of rejection caused by his bizarre behavior. After I'd been in the classroom an hour, there appeared on my desk a valentine hand drawn by Johnny, which simply read, "Mrs. Comp, you're a very nice person. Love, Johnny." Charming and innocent enough, I thought. Then at recess time we played some records because it had started to rain outside and I suddenly found Johnny's hand on my hip engaged in some special hip-hugging maneuvers. I patiently explained, "We do not put our hands on the teacher or anyone else without some understanding that it's ok between the persons." He stormily rushed out of the room shouting, "What's the matter with you? Don't you read the Bible? It says hugs are good for us." I wondered how he had managed to conclude that his attempts to victimize others with intrusive hugs and proddings was blessed and encouraged, and whose biblical interpretation had taught him this behavior.

Another fifth grade boy who proved the "holy terror" of the room on a daily basis, pulled out his copy of AWAKE to "learn about God" during silent reading time set aside for school library books. He was putting the God symbol into yet another act of disruption. He used it often to demonstrate destructiveness in relationships as having the sanction of his interpretation of God.

Repeatedly these youngsters demonstrated being out of touch with self as being born good and able to learn from positive inner signals, as to what was hurtful or helpful to self and others. Instead, they insisted their god symbol would rule the day in the classroom, on the playground, and would continuously rupture relationships, possibly leading them into juvenile hall or even prison. The great hope and blessing for them is that our schools are still democratically oriented and there is an opportunity to learn non-violating behavior from the healthier individuals in their surroundings.

Another form of distorted personal and group power expressed through violence occurred with a high school race riot that broke out on campus where I was teaching classes in Social Studies. Group violence is like a fire that rages mindlessly out of control because it fascinates and compels the participants into wildly letting go of intelligence, compassion and understanding: they discover it is nearly impossible to break out of this compulsion. It is again a demonstration of powerlessness that propels a surrender to violence and this conflict was about to erupt into the use of chains, when two faculty men were able to disperse it temporarily.

At recess time I discovered a senior boy "working his chains", when he volunteered that he "took no crap from no one but would kill first." All these statements and events spoke clearly of the pain and frustration of powerlessness, violations of spirit inflicted by one upon another through ignorance and unawareness that has reached staggering proportions.

Even more amazing was a television documentary on the Los Angeles schools portraying dump trucks in the process of dumping two tons of guns taken from "warring" students in this metropolis. Guns have arrived on our campuses as another expression of the frustrated powers of youth.

Educators cannot continue to impose tunneled, restricted views on the enormous surfacing multidimensional powers of youth. We will either be overwhelmed by these misunderstood energies and possibly forced into burnout, or "silently serve" through our deepening despondency and dissatisfied results with our lives both inside and outside the classroom.

The obvious question is what can an individual teacher do at this time? He/she can begin with examining personal beliefs and the resulting personal reality created as a result of those beliefs. If we see others as "objects to be manipulated", we're in trouble and will reap the results of such tyrannical beliefs and actions. If we view others as born good, potential powerhouses of good, we will be able to celebrate the miracles of transformation, as they occur before our eyes.

People filled with self doubt, afraid of themselves and their inner direction or power seem to live within a framework of hidden beliefs that manifest in accidents, illnesses and ruptured relationships. Fear, anger, and distrust get violently turned against the self. In GAMES PEOPLE PLAY, Eric Berne refers to these events and their extreme results as third degree, hard core gamesmanship. The games revolve around fear and denial of selfhood that can lead to the court, the hospital or the morgue.

Invariably, the greatest source of anger is fearing to make fullest use of one's potential or any consistent commitment to creativity. Fear and distrust of self is, in effect, fear and distrust of one's multidimensional spirit or God within. Whether this denial and fear is consciously contrived through yielding to another's imposed symbols or systems, or due to subconscious hidden beliefs, denial of feelings, perceptions and intuitive nudges, it constitutes a dishonesty that invites continuous suffering. Hurtful projections upon others of dumping and invalidating are destructive concomitant parts of this behavior pattern.

New and broader frameworks of beliefs are crucial to a renewed trust in self and survival of our democratic institution of education. Violations of the self or others have often resulted in extreme violations or violence. Ignoring, blaming, rushing, invalidating and denying selfhood continues to usher many teachers and students to the brink. Current rules and curriculum are often proving too rigidly tunneled and destructive. Too many times a wall of indifference is erected against student discovery of roots, values and purpose. As one cynical Junior High School boy blurted out during a discussion of the golden rule, "He who has the gold makes the rules!" Another pointed out that his creative writing course was only a series of exercises out of the text, a "ripoff" that never allowed them to state what was on their minds and in their hearts.

It's apparent that unless teachers realize and rebel against this kind of ripoff to selves and students, the illness, burnout and accident ratio can only escalate. Fortunately, democratic practice and understandings of continuing consciousness expansion are too widespread to allow tunneled vision to endure.

Personal hidden beliefs are now more easily identified through listing energy drains and guilts as these are invariably tied into artificial guilts or someone else's "shouldedness". It is obvious that violations against each other often lead to a kind of conditioned violence. What teachers often unwittingly pass onto young people consists of daily violations by denying or invalidating their potential. Teachers need to strive for a fuller awareness of this behavior and their roles in it, in order to work themselves out of it.

When creative abilities and potential are not respected nor responded to with encouraging opportunities, granting space for inner vision to express, all are aware of this betrayal of time and energy on some deeper level. Richard Simmons recently pleaded on his therapy exercise program for overweight, anxious persons, "Please don't waste a single minute being any less than you are!", empathizing his understanding of the challenge. His plea again is to stop denying selfhood in an effort to curb anxiety.

I found the syndrome of teacher "wipeout" to be powerfully illustrative of allowing self love and trust to succumb to the artificial guilt that dominated one's point of view or choice in the now moment. Jane Roberts' Seth Literature and similar viewpoints repeatedly remind us that our third dimensional reality is a school where we have an opportunity to learn how to not suffer. Many now recognize and seek non-suffering through wise actions as a main goal or "opportunity" of physical existence.

Because many teachers are determined to put forth a good image in doing a conscientious job, a frequent cause of handicap or attrition is the tendency to drive one's self almost mindlessly at times. This kind of personal violation reaps painful consequences and is often blindly referred to as "dedication". For example, a teacher who required leg surgery kept postponing it because of what she describes as "dedication to completing a testing program." She had convinced herself that simple microsurgery was all that was needed and would not require more than two weeks at home. Two weeks, unfortunately, turned into a painful isolation of nine months, and she is still having difficulty walking.

I could list numerous examples but refrain for the sake of preserving privacy and friendships, but haven't we all known persons who procrastinate or "overload their circuits" causing needless suffering. The suffering of many teachers indicates that we need to continually ask ourselves when feeling driven "out of touch" with real feelings, - -how do we sensibly put the brakes on our runaway guilt? How do we get in touch with what we are feeling and creating right now? Changing probabilities or a part of our reality that is painful or dissatisfying provides us with proof that we can change or create new reality. We must be willing to assume responsibility for focusing direction and consciousness.

In order to function clearly and powerfully, it is essential to look carefully at our hidden behavior and our hidden beliefs; we must learn to recognize and face the guilt, fear and anger that can short circuit our probabilities manifesting as we wish. But we must first be able to clarify these feelings by asking the question, "How do I feel right now?" Next, one needs to ask what is it I want to change or create. What is my top priority. After getting clear with that, it is important to visualize it five minutes daily. This causes a biological repatterning within that propels the probability to manifest. Hidden beliefs can be reprogrammed with simple repetitive statements as, "I deserve loving abundance now", which means never driving the body mercilessly in order to express the power that is already there. We are assured and can discover that when ideas about ourselves change, so will our experiences!

The question of how well any teacher can or would willingly get self out of the way as a "high priest" of education also kept recurring. The belief that somehow I own these kids for the next year; they are mine to be shaped to my tapes and there is no need to consider their "source" because I am it for now. This attitude too often contaminated teacher-student relationships.

As one principal bullied, "These parents are easily cowed." Another teacher agreed, "These parents will do anything to please me." They admit taking advantage of the parents' gullibility in surrendering power, to further manipulate the children according to their conveniences, which too often are blind to respecting the child's inner blueprint. They fail to respect and nurture the creative potential within and lose another opportunity to truly educate.

Gifted youngsters are particularly vulnerable to betrayal for their 4-year "sentencing" to high school boredom and denial of who they are for the sake of the system's desperately prized Average Daily Attendance reports. That stark formula bottom lines into "no bodies – no paychecks".

A particularly intuitive and psychic young man who had been a guest speaker at one of my summer conferences on creativity and psychic development had a motorcycle collision that ended his life. This accident occured the following year shortly after he had confided to his girlfriend how completely bored he felt with entrapment in the sterile psychic environment and phoniness of his high school.

The   prevalent attitude seems to be , who cares what their needs are and how poorly or how well the curriculum meets them. Let's get their bodies in here for counting and pick up our paychecks, because what really matters is meeting our next mortgage and car payment – and all participants suffer.

Because of my understanding of the system and my alert responses to the needs of my children, I was able to intervene in events that might have proven disastrous for my son. On leaving Junior High School, David had requested an advance science class in Senior High because his grade indicated he could handle this challenge. Believing that he would get into some eagerly sought understanding of physics and chemistry, he was dismayed to find himself with a group of slow learners, all of them graduating seniors, who heaped abuse on him, because he was the youngest student present. He was kicked, spit on, his hair pulled and the daily ugliness continued with his teacher never seeming to notice.

David likes to think of himself as one who can handle his own problems and has repeatedly demonstrated this faith in self as well justified. He began cutting class without complaining to anyone. He was, of course, given many detentions at which point I had to appear for a conference with his teachers and administrators. My first question was, "If you can't hold onto your gifted, who owns the problem?" The conference revealed that he found at least two of his classes degrading. In his P.E. class there was no shower supervision and again, he found himself being forced to encounter daily indignities in being sprayed with deodorant, smacked with towels and forced to encounter vulgarities from older, violent students. There was no supervision, because one P.E. teacher was assigned to a class containing over 40 boys, with several of them behavior problems.

Fortunately his math teacher was a family friend who volunteered at this conference to be David's advisor. Like many of our youth, David was without a father due to a divorce when he was ten years old, so this befriending by male teachers was highly significant and helpful. He was also befriended by a history teacher who enjoyed playing tennis with him Saturday mornings and sometimes after school in between tournaments. He usually bought him Saturday breakfast as well. The caring of these men helped steady a shaky environment for David.

But many others must feel the degradation without teacher interest or friendship or endure an even more painful state of powerlessness perhaps leading to dropping out and not receiving a diploma. How many are indeed opting for this in place of the feeling of imprisonment and indifference to who they are and to what they can accomplish.

Who really gives a damn? – is the burning and perplexing question of many students. The teachers are not entirely to blame. The two men who helped David were also recently divorced, pressured with personal and societal problems and seeking their own solutions to complex lives that seemed to be blowing apart, with little or no anchorage. Who owns the problems, indeed? We need to get on with discovering why we are seemingly at the mercy of forces that appear to entrap and destroy our relationships and our youth with increasing accidents, alcoholism, drugs and suicides. First of all, we need to know ourselves more intimately and accept responsibility for directing our consciousness and energies through new understanding and broader frameworks of action.

CHAPTER 9

RESPONSIBLY RESPONDING TO FEELINGS OF POWERLESSNESS IN YOUTH

Our cultural systems tend to use dumping, blaming, denial, invalidation and finally annihilation when feeling unenlightened, confused and fearful. Unless educators will seek for more complete answers, which includes persistent questioning and paying attention to surrounding events, the impasse will continue.   Why has this occurred? What am I doing in the midst of this devastating reality? Or how come I'm so lucky to have joyous, loving, interesting and caring friends and have things work out so well in my life? Is it really luck or did I help create it?

Teachers need to be constantly vigilant as to whether their techniques, methods and approaches help put the young increasingly in touch with their positive inner direction or whether their approach is one of denial and invalidation so that what they do and say comes between youth and its inner awareness.

Education can become a meaningful force only if it enhances appreciation and exercise of individual free will. It must encourage independent thinking with a deep concern for others. If it continues to play irrelevance, denial games, invalidating those who come for an education, demonstrating an unawareness of ploys that shame the young out of self respect, then it is headed for deeper difficulties.

Needless transitional suffering resulting from seething revolution could find peace more directly as a result of this awareness. Each youngster or teacher can be led and encouraged to interpret his/her agitation (or current state of the confusion-denial syndrome) for self. Aspirations, fantasies, and particularly dreams require clarifying and action. (See p. 115, Exercises and Lucid Dreaming.)

Self honesty requires teachers to take a stewardship of their own inclinations, talents and abilities. They need to realistically assess strengths and weaknesses, and identify those defenses erected against internal signals and to work at eliminating them from daily life. In order to help construct harmonious realities with youth, one needs to understand the "point of power" or choice is in every moment, with every mood or feeling, and clearly choose to NOT suffer. One has a choice to NOT be depressed, angry, traumatized, guilty, fearful, self rejecting or anxious for long, as a reaction to problems and life experiences. Helping youth meet their higher needs also means helping self to meet these needs. All can find more tranquility with self, thus eliminating the denier, loser mentality.

One of my most unsettling experiences in denial came from a Junior High School "dumping ground" series of classes for slow or disinterested learners called "Agriculture Studies". The teacher had to leave his duties to visit the doctor for treatment of high blood pressure. The classes behaved as though their own out of touch, out of control pressures were about to blow off the roof. Denial of looking at themselves as good, as powerhouses of potential had led them to daily seek the execution of a small gosling, and then fight over who would do the killing for the day. The goslings were a beautiful fluffy golden brood recently hatched in this room as an animal husbandry educational experience. But they had become symbols of a disregard and even hatred of life. On the day I substituted, one of the boys let the cage door drop on a gosling, breaking its leg with "Oops, we'll have to kill this one, too. The pecking order demands it, or it will be pecked to death."

This occurred almost daily and provided a destructive excitement for the class. I sensed it clearly as a momentary thrill of power over another life form or the opportunity to inflict death.

They also bragged about how they "ran the substitute off " that they had yesterday, and were now a reigning terror with power to do this to anyone. Powerlessness had distorted itself into a runaway violence which would leave them questioning their self respect and worth, increasing their guilt to possible immobilization, depression, or one of the current forms of youthful suicide –accidents, alcohol or drugs.

The gosling incident clarifies that THE FEELING OF POWERLESSNESS DESTROYS! When our behavior reflects denial of our talents, abilities and potential, it is also self-betrayal, and we are painfully aware of this in deeper levels of our personality. The source of our greatest anger is in not making fullest use of potential, but rather fearing to discover it and take responsibility for it. This can erupt into violent destructiveness. The more we deny ourselves and who and what we are, because we fear ridicule or the sabotage efforts of others, the more confused we become. The oppression can be triggered by external or internal signals.

Other forms of denial are agitation which often develops into hyperactivity or violence; invalidation, which is discounting or doing put-downs on a person or situation; the confusion syndrome which presents as "I can't" or "I don't know" and invariably means "I won't"; overadaptation or placating; doing nothing or using energy to inhibit responses; and finally slipping into incapacitation or annihilation. A refusal to make the decision to discover and use latent talents and abilities leads to a loss of decision making power and overwhelming powerlessness or depression. Violence then erupts towards self or others as a suicidal surrender, translating into self hate which is God hate.

Persons who exhibit a high level of denial are also manifesting high level hostility (whether projected outwards or turned upon the self) because they do not love or trust themselves. Self trust means God trust and self love means God love. It's that simple.

Through knowing ourselves we have the opportunity to learn what God is and to learn and know what love is. This must involve risk taking with our abilities in order to see how unlimited we can be with our creativity and to rejoice at our accomplishments. Most systems ask us to look to the God outside ourselves. We are rarely asked to look to the God within and to experience the essence of our magical beingness and creativity. When we can love and trust ourselves in every way, we are then loving and trusting God in ourselves. We are finally able to learn what love is, and we can trust ourselves in making our own decisions as well as our own mistakes, in our efforts to expand.

Learning to appreciate the cooperative bond with one's inner teachers is a most important component of "activist expansion". While we may not be altogether clear regarding our inner order of events, our inner teachers do have this awareness and assist enormously in presenting timely instruction. The Star Children are well aware of this. This concept was clarified for me with the publication of this book. I had to endure what seemed an agonizing watchfulness and waiting for further connections to be made with other personalities and data before attempting to publish. It taught me an awareized patience as I came to appreciate that without these additions, the book would have considerably less impact.

When opportunities for rejoicing in personal accomplishment and achievement are lacking, individuals often respond with hyperactivity or incapacitation. The frustration and pain blockage can be violently devastating. Educators could play a strong, supportive role in personhood unfoldment that would enormously benefit themselves as well as students. As Seth eloquently clarifies, denial of individuality means denying a part of God's mind; in trying to hide our potential we are hiding God.

When we are spontaneously our creative selves, delighting in our accomplishments, we are loving and blessing ourselves as well as others. But spontaneity must be clearly acknowledged. It is not to be confused with repressed material that may erupt from past "slush fund" buildups into license rather than a kind of risked expression that always knows its own order. It is not bent on invalidations or put-downs. It is also clearly not a forced or frantic expression carrying undertones of disruptive panic. When we are truly spontaneous, good mental and physical health is always maintained.

The more we deny or distort or placate, the less honest our expression becomes, and the more psychopathic we become. Lying, bending or curtailing strong, constructive impulses because we are afraid of what others may think will eventually lead to some kind of mental or physical illness. This oppressiveness is now evident throughout most of our society. The Star Children will not tolerate this and have come to change it.

Other students can turn to the opportunity to use guns, now legitimized as early as the Junior High ROTC program. Guns provide momentary release from the feelings of powerlessness, as the goslings did, in offering an opportunity to inflict death. As I watched these well dressed 15-year olds carting their heavy rifles across the green campus lawn, I was reminded of the Mei Lei massacre of women and children during the Vietnam War and the cart blanc slaughter that occurred at the hands of "boys from fine homes". Guns and war have always served as legitimate outlets for a violated sense of power and personhood.

Another dismaying example of denial and invalidation of personhood occurred in a very well disciplined sixth grade in terms of assignments completed. I was astonished to observe during the lunch hour on a rainy day a couple of girls rehearsing what might best be described as a kind of "go-go dance" and the sudden outraged scream from one of them. I moved across the room to ask what was going on and she whispered her furious reaction, "Smitty grabbed my tit. He goosed me! The whole school does it and the teachers say nothing. Right after lunch, I brought up the issue and explained, "This behavior is sexual abuse of each others' bodies. You are to love and respect yourself and others. If you truly loved yourself, you could not behave this way, so that needs to be your first priority."

One boy yelled out, "Well, what if we all like it?" So I clarified his perceptions asking, "Are you speaking for yourself? The reason this has come up is because several girls reported it as abusive." Then I set what I hoped were firm limits: "It cannot continue while I am in this room, nor should it ever occur."

Attempts to avoid discussing values, particularly with regard to sexual development and responsibility for one's spiritual-biological destiny are frequent. An urgent guideline for my own children in the face of peer pressure, was encouraging them to question whether they felt mature and understanding enough to handle so powerful an experience. Youngsters so eager to "give themselves away" in early sex experience usually feel they haven't much to give in any case. Self respect and reflective thinking are sadly lacking and anger is often a strong motivator.

A form of self-destruction literally occurs if sex is undertaken in puberty. Each child knows or can be made aware of the inner upheaval resulting from the creative thrusting of intellect and intuition. Considerable instability is present and friendly communications would help attune them closely and more comfortably with it so these great energies could be reasonably directed. Sexual experience too early can fragment and divide the personality precisely at the time when the unity of these energies is crucial and when optimum clarity is sorely needed, since clarity is power. Intellect and intuition are complementary powers and urgently need to remain intact at this time, or once again, everyone loses – society as well as the children.

Our media pressure young people into feeling that their identity and power is dependent on early sexual performance. I especially value the dream sharing of my daughter, Suzi, on this issue after we discussed and even argued the appropriate age for her to wear lipstick. The dream portrayed herself with best friend, Lori, enjoying themselves on some park swings, laughing and singing with the carefree spirit of children. An elderly man came strolling by, smiling and nodding to them. He lovingly cautioned them to not take down their swing sets too early, but to allow themselves plenty of time to grow up. Happily she followed his advice and today demonstrates a satisfying control of her life and abilities. She chose Pediatric nursing as a career, and lately received an award for Distinguished Nurse of the Year.

Dream communications as well as our daily existential symbols deserve acknowledgement and encouragement as they are potent guides for our lives. The more carefully we pay attention to these symbols and messages, the easier our lives become in creating probabilities. Writing them down makes correlations easier to see, understand and control. Children suffering from leukemia and cancer in Dr. Gerald Jampolsky's Attitudinal Clinic in Tiburon, California discovered that in order to control or stop "scary dreams"- - -"It is important to know that your mind can choose to have a dream any way you want."   A child dreaming about a scary lion would only need to say "Stop!" This is an example of lucid dreaming.

The kind of beliefs we are living are evident in our classroom gestalts which proclaim operant beliefs louder and more clearly than any amount of explaining, verbal or written, ever could. To illustrate, I include three contrasting groups: one dramatizes the beliefs of children effectively leading and instructing the teacher. I've often puzzled over the classroom group gestalt that begins in kindergarten and remains an instructive inspiration to the teacher who luckily "inherits" them.

Recently I enjoyed experiencing a second grade class with this fine reputation and was amazed and delighted with their behavior in the classroom as well as in the library, where they had earned four leadership awards. They were self assured, highly cooperative , a racially mixed group that felt very secure with themselves and each other.

They displayed an inner direction that radiated a comfortable self-confidence. Most appeared to be strongly self-directed from an early age. One boy lost no time in going to the stereo earphones to learn new math formulas and experiment with computers. All possessed an unusual eagerness to learn and cooperate.

By way of contrast, two sixth grade teachers were dealing with different sets of problems and perceptions at age 12 and the influence of each of these men was evident in their classes. The first sixth grade was in a state of noisy bedlam the moment the bell rang. They required very firm limits and seemed unable to calm down except for a period of silent reading. The faculty referred to it as one "having lots of energy", but it is more accurately described as hyper and mis-directed based on unidentified passivity which created an atmosphere of emotional off-shooting or chaos.

Again the most obvious violations of each other in this class were the many power tripping games in evidence. From recess behavior, it became clear that much of the uneasiness centered around a discomfort with one's body and bodily feelings. A state of disruptive, unfulfilled power needs ruled. One child complained that she felt "compelled" to follow the dominant chaotic feeling of this class. "Jennie always turns around and tells me to yell at Kathy, so I had to do it back to her." From this restless class also emerged the two accusing 12-year-old girls whose attempted power tripping with the destiny of an innocent custodian led to the courts and finally to their referral to a guidance counselor.

Again dittoes predominated along with lacks of self-understanding. I attempted a discussion on dream symbols, and suggested a writing and art assignment to clarify these. Joan was suddenly alive with new interest in sharing how her grandfather had visited her after his death, explaining to her why he had chosen to leave and how much happier he felt with his new locale and friends. I shared a similar dream story of my daughter experiencing a visit from her grandmother, who lovingly consoled her after two days of tears and distress. She came by to take Suzi for a drive in her car and drove to a dilapidated house in the country. Pointing to it, she said with much love and gentleness, "You see how tired that old house is, darling? Well, that's how grandma feels about being in her body and I just had to leave now." Next day Suzi's eyes shone radiantly with the comfort she had experienced from her grandmother's closeness and the vivid reality of her dream.

The following week when I was back on the school campus, Joan came running up to me welcoming, "O, you're back. I hope you have a good day!" These children seem to cry out for something more meaningful and powerful to occur during their classroom hours. Why should they put in so much "enforced time" for such boring results. The dream world is a reality that could also easily be utilized for teaching compassion, love, understanding and creative relating.

Another sixth grade was led by a teacher who repeated consistently that self love and self trust were all important to healthy growth. Even if much of the subject matter wasn't remembered, practicing love and trust were more vital to growth and relationships. It was a marvel to visit this room of initially extreme behavior problems and observe how these children obviously felt closer to the source of their own power. They felt good and more at peace with themselves and could extend warmth and courtesy to me easily.

These youngsters had a reputation for being highly unmanageable when Mr. Kay became their teacher. At the end of the semester, this class was a delight to visit. They had achieved a significant turnabout in behavior and several observers commented that "he had brought them a long ways from where they were" when he first inherited them.

They showed much interest in my definition of intuition as a "sudden popping of thoughts in one's head". I also suggested that before falling asleep one might ask to locate lost items or ask for help with any kind of a problem because we all gets lots of help in our sleep state. For example, Tom Edison's biographers tell us he used to catnap in order to dream the solution to an invention. One girl who had lost her shoes had tried this and enthused, "God helps us a lot when we sleep!" Certainly the source of much inspiration and direction comes through dreams and children enjoy and appreciate adults who validate their personal knowledge and discoveries with this "realm".

At the end of the semester, two children confided that, "A couple of you subs were fine, but Mr. Kay is the best!' His outstanding patience and love paid big dividends. He also made a point of emphasizing that no matter how ornery or nasty they had behaved sometime during the day he always told them, "I'll still love you tomorrow." It was his way of expressing unending trust in their better natures, a way of saying, "You were all born good and we all know it.", along with a non-verbal invitation to begin acting it. And not too surprisingly, they usually did.

CHAPTER 10

<u>CONCLUSIONS: STRATEGIES FOR CLASSROOM GESTALT EXPANSION.</u>

I. Actualizing Self Love and Self Trust as God Love and God Trust

Some of the most effective approaches I have used to interest children in their creative power on a one to three day basis as a substitute teacher, were discussing of feelings, symbols, dreams and the sharing of stories portraying the power and magic in ourselves as well as other species, such as the migrating whales and butterflies. Speculation as to who and what guides these migrations allows a glimpse at and appreciation of vast power that involves and embraces all.

Classes often organize for the whale observation boat trip and appreciate being told that the big ocean swells they are likely to encounter   feel like skiing up and down moguls. This adventure necessitates taking a seasick pill the night before and 30 minutes before embarking. (The boat owner also strongly urges this procedure.)

Children enjoy hearing about the whales coming as close as 40 or 50 feet to the boat and doing a breaching leap into the air without having ever upset a boat.

It is a thrilling sight to see these 50 or 60 foot bodies with their ten foot wide tails perform deep sounding dives and then blow an exuberant fountain of water into the air with the skipper yelling the familiar accompaniment, "Thar she blows!"

I wrote the following story of a happy memory which was later published in WHALE TALES by Peter Fromm, under "Transformation and Metaphysics".

"My friend Kathy and I were very excited about going to see the gray whales. A week before we went out, we put in our request to Great Spirit in the Whale Kingdom to have an encounter with the whales.

"I said, 'Beloved whales, we are going to be coming out into the ocean again. Last time one of the mothers came to the boat and showed us her calf, which was a very spiritual experience for me. So, if you dear whales, would just let us meet with you again, we would be so grateful." Having sent out a little prayer to the whales, Kathy and I boarded the boat thinking, or hoping, we would really see a whale.

"The ocean was rough. We were having ten feet swells which threw salt water into our faces. 'Just one breach, that's all I'm asking.' It took about thirty seconds. A whale appeared about a hundred-and-fifty feet off the boat and breached. A woman standing next to me asked how this worked. I told her that projecting vibrations of love and calmness were most effective.

"I demonstrated with a little song: 'Beautiful, beautiful whales, I'll love you forever more.' I urged the other people to just sing a song of appreciation and thanks. 'Just make up anything that lets you project calm, loving vibrations.' They said, 'You lead us in a song!' I said, 'No, no. You each need to do it quietly in your own mind. When we are all doing it together, we are not as calmly focused. Each of you do it.' Almost instantly, a beautiful gray appeared alongside the boat, about a hundred feet off, and breached. The captain announced the whales were in a playful mood, and they had only seen four breaches so far this season.

"We experienced reassuring vibrations and playful antics from the whales for our three and a half hour trip. When the captain said she needed to turn back because we were running out of gas, Kathy said, 'Well, let's ask for a grand finale!'

"I said. 'Oh no. You know anything they give us is from their generosity. I can't ask them again. Think of the energy it takes for a creature the size of a school bus to hurl itself up into the air breaching."

"Her wish was granted. As a final farewell a large whale cut across our bow very slowly. It accompanied us a short way. Some of us were yelling, 'We love you! We thank you!' We felt they had to know how much we cared. This, to us, was clearly a validation of the oneness between all species. As I left the boat, I was astonished when people thanked me. Apparently they felt I had connected them to the whales.

"That night before I fell asleep, I asked to join the whales consciousness in the sleep state. I experienced an electron wavelike cyclical-intermingling of soothing comfort and joy in my dreams."

I encouraged the children to write a story on any of the nature trips or scavenger hunts we would be taking.

I would also offer some general comments on concerns and feelings about why we had come together in this particular way today, and I noted it always smoothed the direction for the day's plan. Usually, I reflect their concerns, pointing out that it takes a little time for us to get used to each other -- "and especially for you to get used to me, a new teacher. I need your help to understand how your class works. Will you help me?" This appeal usually brings forth an immediate flow of good will and cooperation.

Then I add some anecdotes about how I raised a boy and a girl not too long ago, and how they felt about their challenges and opportunities at this grade level, but most importantly, how they discovered they had choice in every minute and in every hour. By age 18, the girl had chosen to be an artist and the boy had chosen to be a computer specialist. A few years later, the girl chose an additional career as a Pediatrics Nurse, and the boy started his own Computer Company. The class usually seemed reassured to hear that others like themselves had made it ok into growing up while coping with similar problems.

I also discovered they were at first a little fearful and possibly angry, sometimes feeling the regular teacher had "deserted" them for the day, and they appreciated having these feelings acknowledged. So I mentioned the golden rule, always emphasizing, "You are all good, beautiful human beings. Some of your abilities are known to you and some more are still hidden and it's always fun to discover more about ourselves. So the story I share will help us think more deeply about that. JONATHAN LIVINGSTON SEAGULL was always a favorite.(See resource books, Pg. 117).

"Most of all it's important and above all else it's necessary to listen to your inner direction or good impulses." Then I stress that , "You need to love and trust yourself really well before you can give or share this with a friend. And no matter what you have said or done in the past, you can always correct course and behave and accomplish in ways you'd really like to.   That's the beauty of choice in every moment!"

Whenever I faced a new group, I was reminded of Seth's wise advice to a clinical therapist that you are not in a teaching or facilitating role with others to play savior to them because only they can choose to do this for themselves; but you are there primarily because you have structured this learning situation for yourself. I knew that all teachers of The Star Children would learn immensely from their gifts. They had come to shift our consciousness to help us change, and will help the planet to move into the new energy of love and peace. Teachers also needed to help these special children be unafraid of their gifts.

As Seth indicated- - -you want to learn from what you have set up for yourself. Immediate feedback was always available in terms of how effectively the class responded to a method , technique or strategy, and how helpful it was to them.

I was intrigued with class loyalties and responses to second grader, Eddy, who was a non-reader and "well tuned out" non-learner. Yet on the way to the bus, several children hugged him and asked to sit with him. He reminded me of an adopted nephew who could not really get with the three R's until the fifth grade, but my children were always eager to sit next to him at holiday family gatherings. His wit, imagination and creative psychic expressions were delightfully spontaneous. Such a child provided unusual and evocative learning experiences which account for his popularity, despite curriculum demands and judgments.

In a particularly quarrelsome fourth grade, I again emphasized self love and self trust and added, "Hopefully, by the time you leave fourth grade you will love and respect yourself and each other at least a little more – no, I mean a whole lot more!"

Jerry, who seemed to be a non-reader, non-hearer and non-thinker suddenly burst into applause. He let us know what was important and made good sense to him. I'd never heard anyone express it with more enthusiasm and need than this fourth grader. I had noticed when working with disturbed children that the fourth grade was a particularly lonely year for most of them. Friends and acceptance were all important and now, ten years later, Jerry was still saying the same thing about his feelings as a fourth grader.

Emphasis on self love and trust and sharing this with others, brought forth still another challenging message from Rachel, a fifth grader. She was referred to by class as a bully, a stealer of pencils and everything else not carefully guarded. She had put her head down on the desk as if in despair of ever achieving such a level of self love and trust. On the playground her behavior exploded into a bullying violence as she sank her nails into one girl and pushed another down. Her feelings of self hatred and deprivation would require firm limits and frequent opportunities to release inner pressures so she might see how to redirect her energy into more positive rewarding experiences. Peer pressure would always work admirably, as her despairing gesture indicated she wanted approval and love but did not know how to accomplish it.

It's often been said, "Without a vision, the people perish." Children are people and it's imperative that they have a vision and experience of themselves as hopeful, joyous, loving constructive co-creators. In this respect, their needs are the same as their teacher's. A turnabout change in behavior is not always possible to achieve within a year's time, but any teacher creating a strong, positive classroom probability through his/her beliefs about self and others can give each extreme behavior problem a strong nudge towards clearly reconnecting with positive inner power.

A second grade creative writing session quickly educated me to the great need children have for strong encouragement and appreciative listening in order to overcome the hesitation and fear of expressing their creative ideas as "worthy of sharing".   I would often encourage them with, "You know what's right for you to share, because you are creative and whatever you say is important."

Younger children demonstrate greater flexibility, sensitivity , openness and trust. They are extremely sensitive barometers to adult feelings and moods, not having been as strongly conditioned in our "competitive tunneled view" culture. Toby was a kindergarten child who acted out his insecurities in several ways, one of which was breaking out of line to run upfront as fast as he could. When I firmly told him to go to the end of the line for running, he expressed his insecurity with my firmness by putting on his cowboy hat and vest. When I had an opportunity to smile and speak more kindly to him in the story circle, he took off these items and put them back with his coat. I've noticed that fear often causes a child to put on a coat or more clothing at once as a kind of security blanket. They are very good at signaling their needs if the teacher cares to tune in and change course. An "awareized" balance needs to be maintained between firmness and gentleness.

First grade Janie loved to draw and also appeared to be a non-reader. After I commented on how well she drew and hugged her, she did remarkably well with her reading lesson.

From the preceding examples, it can be seen that children express emotional hunger needs in a variety of ways and do so more openly and vulnerably in the lower grades. These needs include affection, trust, appreciation, acceptance, belonging, pleasure and understanding, with opportunities to express feelings spontaneously on paper at any time. Again, good mental and physical health would always be maintained if spontaneity were encouraged and accepted.

II. Symbology Application: Sleep State and Waking State Symbols.

Children also enjoy sharing their dreams if given an opportunity. It is the dream world reality that contributes so much to present understandings and problem solving. One child shared that he would "dream something about school and by noon it happened." When he shared this, several others volunteered that they had experienced the same precognitive visioning. This sharing offers support to all that the dream world is indeed valid, highly creative and able to offer suggestions for creating opportunities as well as solving problems. Children need acknowledgement, solidarity and direction with their other dimension experiences and not invalidation, which is often expressed through silence.

Creating dream boxes is a helpful way to experience dreams coming true. The ancient Native Americans would create them by selecting and decorating a special box. They would explain how important it was to visualize your dream. Then write it on a piece of paper and put it in the box. Every day say a prayer for your dream to come true and act as if it already has. It will eventually happen.

It is also helpful to create a dream journal. Sometimes a favorite relative or friend can be summoned . My daughter, Suzanne wept unhappily when her grandmother passed on. (See Pg. 88 for children summoning deceased grandparents.)

Another reality many children remember are out of body trips into the greater universe. One boy shared that "I was high up in the stars and started falling last night." Another girl added, "I felt myself turning round and round before I woke up. It seemed I turned like this before coming back into my body." A little bit of sharing in this manner helps others see that the dream world is not meaningless, silly or chaotic. It also gives all the listening children encouragement to remember and discuss dreams. A fascinating approach to finishing these dreams through daytime imaging exercises is presented in the CENTERING BOOK by Hendricks and Wills. (See Bibliography, pg. 109) Solutions to the problems are often dreamt and pop up as intuitive nudges next day.

Another example of intuitions or "thoughts popping" developed around first grader Jody asking me before I had a chance to meet any of the children, if I knew how to do magic. When I replied, "Sure, we all do." he then asked me to make his box of crayons disappear, but I said I was interested in a different kind of magic, like the kind that makes sudden thoughts pop in your head. I said I would share a story about another young boy named Emir, who had to name the animals of the earth and when he met a brown-green log in the swamp, the name "alligator" just popped up as it opened its jaws and showed all its teeth.

Later that day when the class went to have pictures taken in the cafeteria, Jody was suddenly drawn to a table with a drawer, as the thought popped, "That drawer needs opening." Inside he found several cartons of sour milk that needed to be thrown away. He was able to discover and root out the source of this overpowering smell before it got to be too much! He enjoyed this example of intuitive knowing, or "thoughts popping", and after we talked about it, said he'd like to pay closer attention.

One of the most powerful uses of the sleep state is to resolve conflict or fighting with neighbors or family members. In this way no one gets hurt. Suzi, at age 12, had a falling out with a neighbor girl, Rudy, and had been threatened by her "ganging up" after school. That night before falling asleep she asked to have this resolved in her sleep. She dreamt that as she left and went to the garage, "Rudy came along and said something to me which led to her throwing a punch. So I grabbed her fist and put my foot on her legs. She said, "Tomorrow a party", which meant a fight and I said, "No, no party. One of us will get wiped out, and so no party." It sounded like a good enough reason and we were both smiling. Then I opened the garage door and walked home." Next day, no ganging up on Suzi occurred as had been originally threatened. In this manner, children can be taught that physical violations of fighting and warfare are unnecessary, which is what the Senoi people of Central Malay Peninsula have done for centuries. They have experienced no warfare for over 200 years, and they believe and respond to the dream state as very real indeed.

When one can come to accept one's personal magic in creating reality and can learn powerfully from attention to daytime symbols, as well as dream symbols, a whole new exciting world of learning opens up. In a Special Education class I was again sharing my favorite story of EMIR'S EDUCATION IN THE PROPER USE OF MAGIC POWERS by Jane Roberts, explaining how he was having a dialogue and temper tantrums with the universe demanding "no rain" for his boat trip. By way of affirmation a shooting star crossed the heavens. Playfully, I asked the class if anyone had ever had a talk with the sky and seen a shooting star. One boy who suffered poor coordination shared that last month he asked the sky to help him "not wreck up his bike again", and then he saw one. Pushing his luck, he then asked that the world not be flooded with water again, and this time he saw two stars cross each other as a kind of double assurance.

The class was delighted to hear of these new possibilities. I further reinforced the validity of his experience explaining that when I first tried to write this book, I was looking for assurance that it should be helpful for people and not just a waste of my time. A shooting star also responded to this thought which encouraged me enormously. In this kind of playful sharing, children are supported in their hope that some kind of powerful caring always surrounds them. Most were curious enough to want to try the shooting star experiment.

In another fifth grade, two boys shared they were camping out at a nearby lake and wished to catch some fish the next day. They each saw a shooting star as they were speaking of their hopes, and the following day each caught his limit.

Another delightful surprise occurred in a second grade where children were making leprechaun puppets, using a paper design for St. Patrick's Day. I asked jokingly if they thought it possible to really see these little folks as some Irish people believe, or is the leprechaun just a make-believe character?

Bud and Billy eagerly shared they had been sitting in Billy's room one day after school, looking at his window garden box, when they spied a little green man sitting under a mushroom. When he turned to nibble on a carrot green they could not contain their enthusiasm and their shouts brought Billy's mother into the room. At this point, the little figure disappeared. Billy insists he had seen him fleetingly, once before, sitting under the mushroom, when Bud had not been present. The shared and sincere excitement of these two boys made me pause to wonder why adults are so eager to invalidate these experiences. I chuckled with delight at their being joyously involved with sharing other dimensional experience. Clearly many teachings are "happening" to young people that are not in the curriculum.

A most inspiring sharing came from an unusually sensitive and aware child in a Special Education Class. After I finished reading a story entitled "Three Wishes", I asked the children what their wishes might be if they could have anything at all. Tina replied, "I wish I could get to know God." I asked, "What does that mean to you ?" Her remarkably enlightened answer was, "Know the people and what they need!"

Not all symbolic sharing was this cheering. A most perplexing series of day-time symbols occurred in a kindergarten where one boy shared his experience of being in an automobile accident. He had been hurled through a window which resulted in his face being badly cut. Several others were then eager to share their fearful accidents. I asked for a counting of hands to see how many had been similarly involved, and was astonished to observe that more than one-fourth of these children had already shared in this trauma by age 6. There are obvious profound family lessons occurring with these events, from which the teacher can also learn.

For a change to joyous symbology, a guided imagery fantasy called the Hot Air Balloon Trip can be introduced.   This exercise gives the children a chance to fly while visualizing their fondest dreams or wishes and attuning to ways to make them happen. (See Appendix of Exercises, Pg. 113) For example, one child wanted a 10-speed bike that his parents could not afford. The following week, his neighbors moved to Hawaii and were happy to sell him a 10-speed for just $5. Teachers can offer many more examples if they attune.

III.   Assimilating Broader Creativity Frameworks.

A consideration of the following concepts and questions offer powerful keys to changing beliefs and restructuring classroom gestalt relationships:

Teacher beliefs regarding self are always reflected in classroom results. Could teachers be open to trusting, (in addition to teacher training methods), their own intuitive nudges or creativity fluctuations while communicating with children in groups or on a one-to-one basis? Could they joyously and playfully program themselves to believe in self love and self trust, learning to grow in the awareness that they are unlimited powerhouses of potential for creative expression and problem solving? Or would they at least be able to work at demonstrating this irreversible "consciousness expansion" potential to self by recording results of symbology attunement and goals or ideals actualized? Programming one's dreams for problem solving and conflict resolution and then recording the results has proven an invaluable encouragement resource.

Several guideline books are available to teachers who are open and willing to develop other dimensional assistance. (See Bibliography: Books by Roberts, Hendricks, Rozman, Pg. 113)

Most importantly, choice in the NOW moment needs to be valued and practiced as the essential actualizer. "Aliveness awareness" includes lists of joyous activities as well as energy drains, and this included attunement to feelings that powerfully affect the physical body. Planetary chaos and threat call for carefully structured hours of joyous choices in order to be centered most of the time.

The teacher would be inspired in validating the internal, intrinsic joy of learning and encourage each child towards closer communication with self or personhood by asking any and all questions that fascinate the child, by encouraging sharing of feelings and wishes or goals on a regular basis and offering a variety of creativity triggers such as drawing, painting, creative writing, poetry (song lyrics) and music. The keeping of a creative journal (once the trust of the child has been earned) as a deconditioning process to the usual restrictive "official curriculum", exploring correlations between dreams symbols and daily events . This practice would put the child closer to "Who am I and what am I doing here? What do I hope to gain?" By encouraging the child to see and feel what s/he already deeply knows, thus cooperating with the child's inner blueprint, one can create an exciting, developing classroom gestalt of learning. Such learning opportunities put everyone closer to their inner direction in terms of roots, values, and purpose.

Through their dream symbols, children are often being shown who they are, and what they can accomplish, despite oppressive, dull classroom curriculum. For example, Suzi at age six, was reassured of her powerful abilities as a speaker and guide through her artistic expression and "flock of colors" in a precognitive dream. " We were in this weird place called Bethlehem and we had to live in a little shelter. And so I went into my room and it was very dark. And suddenly a big flock of colors came. And suddenly it spoke to me and then I knew it was God. And so it spoke one more time and said, 'I hate myself'. And so I drew a picture of God, and God just liked to keep it that way. But then I said, 'God come back.' And God did come back. God was mad at himself for how the world was going, so it just wanted to be a scribbled up piece of paper and it was going to throw itself into the fire.

"But I said, 'God, if you do that, what will happen to everything? What will happen to all the people who believe in you? Everything will be in the fire.' And God turned on all the colors cause I was God's friend. And I think that was the best dream I ever had."

As a high school graduating senior, she wrote some intimate thoughts, quoting from a song that men of high places must now "mold a reality closer to the heart," asking dreams, won't you show me the way? This challenge includes the nation's educators as well as its statesmen. The thrust of this energy and these messages from waking and sleep state symbols will continue whether policymakers are willing to heed them or not. It is truly counterproductive to oppose or not seek to cooperate with so beneficent and enormous a power. Natural consequences of choices and decisions regarding any policy will structure future events in terms of erroneous stagnation or expansion.

Suzi later became a glass painter with a profitable website,. where she sold paintings ranging from $600 to $1000. Some of these can still be viewed on the Internet.

Recognizing that consciousness expansion IS healthy survival would largely eliminate numerous restrictive dittoes to inner expression, whether in the arts, or creating opportunities and solving problems from a unique personal perspective. There would be time to pursue those concepts that fascinate. Teacher-child relationships would constantly be restructured into more cooperative and loving understandings. Allowing the child to experience more fully inner strengths and resources would draw the teacher into a keener appreciation of the beauty and power of each, thereby increasing his/her capacity for loving and trusting self as well as the other selves in that room. It would be a reciprocal circle of growth that eliminated misunderstanding and guilt over lost opportunities to learn. Children could be led to feel safe in sharing the deeper levels of their creative selves, no matter now brutal other areas of their environment might be. Resistances to learning would disappear as a more positive cooperation and eagerness to learn surfaced. The sharing of feelings, dreams and creative choice DOES create such a climate.

The expression of joyous creativity powerfully expressed would be an exciting ongoing daily growth "happening" for each. But such a developing gestalt must rest on the firm foundational belief that each of us is born good and yearns for an on-going opportunity to express inner ideals, no matter how discouraging one's present family background or present life conditions. We are each worthy of being "heard". The Star Children insist on it.

An awareness centered assignment for teaching global harmony is, "In my world I am born good, and this is what I would change or create." This can be done with a 5-minute period for silent reflection followed by oral sharing as a starter, leading into creative writing. I have been thrilled with the variety of inner responses to this exercise from individuals in my classes on "Creativity and Psychic Development". It is an excellent training practice for would be global futurists.

Individuals must be willing to love and trust self sufficiently to demonstrate to themselves the magic unfoldment of who they are. No other teachers, groups or books can do it for us. Teachers can prove supportive IF they help the individual to actualize ideals.

It has often been said, "As we learn to meet the needs of our children, so shall we learn to meet our own." Richard Bach's JONATHAN LIVING SEAGULL proudly points to the accomplished high flyers he experienced in experiencing their latent flying abilities, emphasizing that they were not special, gifted or divine, but rather, they had begun to understand what they really were and to practice it. He heartily encourages all of us to take that next step forward into creative expansion.

Creativity or choice, resourcefulness in identifying passivity behavior, joy and spontaneity can be structured into any classroom gestalt, and would reflect the developing perceptions of each person in that room. A new willingness to "hear", respect and creatively encounter each other is a simultaneous development of this loving and trusting process. The self image of all participants becomes strengthened as they realize that what they say and feel is worth sharing and being listened to or truly "heard". A glowing reaffirmation of selfhood is the positive result. The Star Children will encourage their classmates in sharing what they already know as "their mission".

Children yearn to know that no matter what they have said or done they were born good or in a state of natural grace, and that their bodies are good. They are continuing in this state because no one has the power to invalidate it or take it away. An example of natural grace expressed physically is the replacement of our cells every seven years. No one keeps track, yet it occurs. Babies learn to crawl and walk, not because their parents teach them, but because a set of internal signals tells them it's time to do so.

Children also need to be taught to NOT empower the projections of others who are unwittingly laying their guilt trips and communicating destructive put-downs rather than encouraging creativity. Teaching children assertiveness or limit setting to the bully behavior of others is another essential. "No bullies and no doormats", is a goal simply established and consistently examined. The overall goal is non-acceptance of the destructive projections of others and no surrendering of power.

Children can also be helped to examine the intent of another's words, asking, "How do these words make me feel?" With a little practice, they can quickly see through the manipulations and projections of another. Star Children are very adept at this.

Children also need practice with exercising individual choice and discovering that parts of reality with which they are not satisfied CAN be changed. Singing THE MUPPET MOVIE hit, "Can You Picture That?" provides excellent reinforcement , and encourages the imaging or visualizing necessary for a new manifestation.

They need guidance in realizing that clarity is power and to visualize what they wish to happen in their world or relationships after first getting very CLEAR with their desire. Visualizing for five minutes daily will cause a desired reality to begin manifesting in 21 days or less. Emotional intensity is a powerful key in this process. All can discover the primary rule of co-creating is that we get what we focus upon. Underlying or hidden beliefs also need to be changed when they hamper a willingness to assume responsibility for "directing consciousness", which in turn becomes part of a larger network directing even greater power.

Beliefs can be readily understood and changed through releasing and tracing feelings of hurt, fear and anger, thus learning to love and trust ourselves in every way. To recognize, face and replace our negatives with positive energy is the magical liberating key in this process. It allows us to glimpse a clearer sense of direction of purpose. Integrating one's self and belief structures to achieve inner trust is an essential first step in this process.

In the first grade, Tommy was assured that painting out his native feelings was an appropriate and acceptable channel for release of his pent-up agitation. Prior to this acceptance, he had not been able to sit still in the sharing circle but rolled restlessly across the floor. A miraculous breakthrough in understanding occurred with his first attempts at painting a smeary kind of brown and blue prison with black bars. This represented his home life and harsh treatment by his father.

It was quickly followed by his first painting of identifiable persons and objects. He had portrayed himself in a purple suit playing outside on a sunny day. The sun was still encircled by a black ring, but essentially the picture was an optimistic, rejoicing statement that he had clearly left his prison behind. I felt tears welling up as I watched this child's miraculous breakthrough unfold.

Brent was also a deeply disturbed child struggling to work his way out of a painful emotional maze. I was introduced to him in a clinical setting as an encopretic, enuretic controlling child. His refusal to go to the bathroom was his way of attempting to fight back at the over-controlling adults in his life. Every day for a month, he went through sandbox battle scenes, along with dollhouse play, drawings and paintings, which gave him the opportunity to vent his fears and rage. The turning point came when he picked up the telephone in the dollhouse one day and said to me, trustingly, "Can you direct me?" Throughout the summer I worked with him, he had remained dry and cooperatively used the bathroom indicating again the universal need and healing power of human freedom, when allowed its expression of spontaneity and autonomy.

Mark was another child trapped in a maze of poor physical coordination. He appeared to be accident prone and one day confided that he was seeing a man in a white uniform without feet who called himself "the professor" and promised to help guide him in coordinating his physical body. This child was a close friend and neighbor and the following Christmas season I had the privilege of teaching him to ski. With total amazement, I watched him take the chair lift alone, after one short lesson, get off without falling and ski down an unusually long beginner's slope without mishap. When he got to the bottom of the hill, his mother and I greeted him with cheers and noticed he appeared to be somewhat dazed. I asked him eagerly if he wished to try the run again. "No," he replied somewhat dazed, "I've got to sit down and think about what happened." It seemed "the professor" had taken a hand in guiding him and helping him coordinate, but Mark never forgot that first courageous episode and today remains a non-accident skiing enthusiast.

These are some examples of multi-dimensional personhood manifesting in seemingly miraculous ways. They are still based on inner trust, or a willingness to heed the messages of inner direction.

In conclusion, the main goal or purpose is to help put children in touch with their multi-dimensional personhood. There is no education that can be considered truly valid without doing so. Opportunity for expansion is the crying need of the day, not policies of repression. The Indigo and Crystal children must have a flexible teaching environment. The Indigo "system busters" of the education system have made that very clear. All children want to use their psychic abilities, including their dream power, and at least glimpse how the universe works. The ultimate reward is coming to know, through a variety of experiences, that individual creativity is unlimited and that we were born to "express the great joy and spontaneity of our nature".

For the sake of clarity, I include a synopsis of an effective 5-step classroom format for such accomplishment:

1.   It is first necessary to guide the children into an appreciation of self love and self trust, rekindling in them that they are born good and are in a state of natural grace which they have never lost;

2.   These realizations are essential to sharing feelings and symbols from both the sleep state and waking state to clarify direction and purpose; they also accelerate and deepen understanding, forgiveness, sharing and supporting, -- interchanging with others. Choice in the NOW moment is an essential actualizer and rejuvenator for directing emotional energy intelligently, and needs to be consistently exercised. This calls for frequent reminders and opportunities to practice.

3.   The process of choosing also requires an awareness of passivity behaviors. Questions that keep us closely in touch with self are: How do I feel right now? Am I discounting self, another person or situation, and insisting on a state of powerlessness? Why?

4.   Finally, learning to trust the deeper levels of the group gestalt and one's dreams reminds us of the magic of our creativeness. It provides stability and tranquility while directing us towards a deepening spirituality throughout joyous, loving thoughts and behavior. The gestalt, with its frequent surprise solutions, helps eliminate artificial guilt and confusion, while putting us in intimate touch with our multi-dimensional network.

It is never too late to learn from our personal hidden beliefs, to change course and to direct our mental and emotional power towards a more holistic outcome with our children. More satisfying realities with far less suffering will be brought about because of such an effort. When we forget we are "the magic", hidden beliefs continue to structure painful situations of grief and sorrow. This continues until we remember who we are, and begin to take responsibility for creating or changing our reality.

Once children become aware that they are the magic, they need opportunities to determine what is fascinating and worth questioning. Impulse attunement becomes a primary guide. It cannot be said too often that all want and need to express their inspiring inner heroics, which are messages from the psyche or soul.

The Indigo Children have come as a catalyst to show us what is wrong and what must be changed. They have come knowing what their mission is. As beings of higher abilities, they will teach us a new politics.

Politics had usually meant to me a form of control over another, whether that pertained to family members, the pecking order within systems, or global nations. The Indigos symbolize strong autonomy for each person understanding that real power is the force of mind plus the great energy of the emotions intelligently directed; and always with a compassionate concern for others. They will insist on an understanding of tolerance and cooperation in everything they do. Some will most probably become presidents, governors and lawmakers. Primarily, they will focus on education and health care as these directly impact their lives.

This new politics means encouraging and granting each other space for clearly understanding and directing the great power within. I have no doubt that most children will learn to actualize this power into new visions and solutions to the ecosystem problems of climate change, overpopulation, war, food/unsustainable agriculture, quality and quantity of water, war, and energy, and violations of one another, that presently elude our policy makers.

We may indeed look forward to the manifesting of this creativity into a future that will benefit all creatures, great and small. This is why the Star Children have arrived. They will help direct us into a world whose new understandings have freed humankind from racist and sexist prejudice, a world without war, but with enlightened harmony manifesting in a reverence for all forms of consciousness and personalities. These children carry a new vibration that will transform the consciousness of humanity. They are the children of oneness and they function as a group consciousness, living by the "law of global oneness."   With immense gratitude, those of us who are aware of their gifts, welcome the Star Children and all they have to teach us.

BIBLIOGRAPHY

Chapter One

1. Sawyer, Diane , You Tube, ABC News Interview of Indigo Family.

2. Rodwell, Mary, AWAKENING, HOW EXTRATERRESTRIAL CONTACT CAN TRANSFORM YOUR LIFE, Fortune Books, Great Britain, 2000.

3. Ibid

4. Chapman, Wendy and Flynn, Carolyn, COMPLETE INDIOT'S GUIDE TO INDIGO CHILDREN, Penguin Group, Alpha Books, Indianapolis, IN, 2007.

5. Ibid

6. Varmun, Keith, SUPER PSYCHIC KIDS, You Tube Demonstration.

7. Melchizadek, Drunvalo, THE NEW DNA, You Tube Lecture.

8. Geller, Uri, TV Demonstration, Keith Varmun, You Tube.

9. Patillo, Nikki, CHILDREN OF THE STARS, ADVICE FOR CHILDREN AND PARENTS, Huntsville, AR, 2008.

10. Virtue, Doreen, Ph.D, THE CRYSTAL CHILDREN, Hay House, NY, 2003

11. Rodwell, Mary, AWAKENING, HOW EXTRATERRRISTRIAL CONTACT CAN TRANSFORM YOUR LIFE, Great Britain, Fortune House, 2000.

12. Ibid

13. Dong, Paul & Rafill Thomas, CHINA'S SUPER PSYCHICS, Marlowe & Co., 1997.

14. UCLA Medical Research on New DNA, 2010.

15. Day, Peggy and Gale, Susan, PSYCHIC CHILDREN, A SIGN OF OUR EXPANDING AWARENESS, A.R.E. Press, 2004.

16. Dancoes, Dumari, Comments, You Tube.

17. Patillo, Nikki, CHILDREN OF THE STARS, ADVICE FOR CHILDREN AND PARENTS, Huntsville AR, 2008.

18. Clark, Arthur, CHILDHOOD'S END, Ballantine Books, 1953.

19. Dancoes Dumari, Comments, You Tube.

20. Virtue, Doreen, Ph.D, THE CRYSTAL CHILDREN, Hay House, NY, 2003.

21. Virtue, Doreen Ph.D., CD/INDIGO, CRYSTAL AND RAINBOW CHILDREN, 2010.

22. Virtue, Doreen, Ph.D. THE CARE AND FEEDING OF INDIGO AND CRYSTAL CHILDREN, Hay House, NY, 2010.

23. Virtue, Doreen Ph.D. CD/INDIGO, CRYSTAL AND RAINBOW CHILDREN, Hay House, NY, 2010

24. Chapman, Wendy & Flynn, Carolyn, THE COMPLETE IDIOT'S GUIDE TO INDIGO CHILDREN, Penguin Group, Alpha Books,Indianapolis, IN, 2007.

25. Ibid

Chapter 2

Brezsny, Rob, PRONOIA, North Atlantic Books, Berkeley, CA, 2009.

2. Arguelles, JOSE, EARTH ASCENDING, "The Transformative Vision", Bear & Co., Santa Fe, NM, 1988.

Chapter 4

1.   Dong, Paul & Rafill, Thomas, CHINA'S SUPER PSYCHICS, Marlowe & Co. 1997.

2.   Roberts, Jane, SETH SPEAKS, Prentice Hall, Inglewood Cliffs, NJ, 1974.

3.   Goldman, Burt, QUANTUM JUMPING, Mind Valley, LC, 2010.

4.   Chapman, Wendy and Flynn, Carolyn, THE COMPLETE IDIOT'S GUIDE TO INDIGO CHILDREN, Penguin Group. Indianapolis, IN, 2007.

5.   Martin, Zak, HOW TO DEVELOP YOUR ESP, Richard Clay, Ltd, Bungay, Suffolk, Great Britain, 1986.

6.   Ferguson, Marilyn, ACQUARIAN CONSPIRACY, J. P. Archer, Pblshr. 1980.

Chapter 5

1.   Brezsny, Rob, PRONOIA, North Atlantic Books, Berkeley, CA, 2009.

Chapter 6

1.   Terkel, Studs, WORKING, New Press, 1997.

Chapter 7

1.   Dyer, Wayne, THE SKY'S THE LIMIT, Simon and Schuster, NY, 1980.

2.   Chapman, Wendy & Flynn, Carolyn, THE COMPLETE IDIOT'S GUIDE TO INDIGO CHILDREN. Penguin Group, Alpha Books, Indianapolis, IN, 2007.

3.   Naumberg, Margaret, AN INTRODUCTION TO ART THERAPY, STUDIES OF THE FREE EXPRESSION IN PROBLEM CHILDREN AND ADOLESCENTS AS A MEANS OF DIAGNOSIS IN ART THERAPY, Teachers' College Press, Coilumbia, NY, 1973.

4.   Bissell, H. and Palomares, U., METHODS IN HUMAN DEVELOPMENT TRAINING INSTITUTE, LAJOLLA, CA. 1960.

5. Brezsny, Rob, PRONOIA, North Atlantic Books, Berkeley, CA, 2009.

6. Tolle, Eckhart, PRACTICING THE POWER OF NOW, New World Library, Novato, CA, 1999.

7.   Jampolsky, Gerald, M.D. BEHIND EVERY CLOUD THERE'S A RAINBOW. Celestial Arts Publishers, Millbrae, CA, 1978.

Royce, et al, ART THERAPY QUARTERLY, NY, 1972.

8.   Kubler-Ross, Elizabeth, M.D., "Life, Death and Life After Death" (Tape) Shanti Nilaya, Escondido, CA, 1980.

9. Axline, Virginia, DIBS, Boston-Houghton Mifflin, 1964.

10. Baruch, Dorothy W. NEW WAYS IN DISCIPLINE, McGraw Hill, 1948.

11. Gordon, Tom, Ph.D. TEACHER EFFECTIVNESS TRAINING, Three Rivers Press, NY, 2003.

12. Maltz, Maxwell, PSYCHOCYBERNETICS, Prentice-Hall, Inc., Inglewood Cliffs, NJ, 1960.

13. Stearn, Jess, POWER OF ALPHA THINKING, Wm. Morrow & Co. Inc, 1976.

14. Dreikurs, Rudolf, CHILDREN THE CHALKLENGE, Duell, Sloan Pierce, Pblshrs, 1964.

15. Roberts, Jane, THE NATURE OF PERSONAL REALITY, Prentice Hall, Inc. Inglewood Cliffs, NJ, 1974.

16. Schneider, Caroline, I KNOW YOU LOVE ME, Joy Publications, P.O. Box 373, Santa Maria, CA, 1981.

17. Moustakas, Clark, LONELINESS AND LOVE, Prentice-Hall, Inglewood Cliffs, NJ, 1972.

Chapter 8

1. Conway, Flo and Siegelman, Jim, HOLY TERROR, Doubleday 1982.

2. Miller, Arthur, THE CRUCIBLE, Penguin Book Piblishers, NY 1976.

3. Berne, Eric, M.D., GAMES PEOPLE PLAY, Ballantine Pblshrs, NY,
1964.

4. Roberts, Jane, NATURE OF PERSONAL REALITY, A SETH BOOK,
Prentice Hall, Inc., NJ, 1974.

Chapter 9

1.   Hendricks, Gay and Wills, Russell, THE CENTERING BOOK,
AWARENESS ACTIVITIES FOR CHILDREN, PARENTS AND TEACHERS,
Prentice-Hall, Inc., Englewood Cliffs, N Jer., 1975.

2. Roberts, Jane, NATURE OF PERSONALILTY, A SETH BOOK, Prentice
Hall, Inc., Inglewood Cliffs, N. Jer., 1974.

3. Ibid

4. Roberts, Jane, NATURE OF THE PSYCHE, ITS HUMAN EXPRESSION, A
SETH BOOK, Chs. 3, 4, Prentice-Hall, Inc., Englewood Cliffs, N Jer.,
1979

Chapter 10

1. Comp, Rita, "Beloved Whales" , in WHALE TALES, VOL 2, collected
by Peter Fromm, Whale Tales Press, Friday Harbor, WA, 2000.

2. Chapman, Wendy & Flynn, Carolyn, THE COMPLETE IDIOT'S GUIDE
TO INDIGO CHILDREN, Penguin Alpha Books, Indianapolis, IN, 2007.

3. Hendricks, Gay and Roberts, Thomas B.,THE SECOOND CENTERING
BOOK; MORE AWARENESS ACTIVITIES FOR CHILDREN, PARENTS
AND TEACHERS, Prentice-Hall, Inc., Inglewood /Cliffs, NJ, 1977.

4.   Roberts, Jane, EMIR'S EDUCATION IN THE PROPER USE OF MAGIC
POWERS, Delacorte Press, Eleanor Friede, NY, 1979.

5. Bach, Richard, JONATHAN LIVINGSTON SEAGULL, Mcmillan Co. NY,
1970.

6. Stewart, Kilton "Dream Theory In Malaya", (Article)1972.

7. Roberts, Jane, NATURE OF PERSONAL REALITY, A SETH BOOK,
Prentice I Hall Inc., Englewood Cliffs, NJ, 1974.

8. William, Paul and Ascher, Kenny, "Can You Picture That?" , Song
from THE MUPPET MOVIE, 1982.

9. Roberts, Jane, NATURE OF PERSONAL REALITY, A SETH BOOK,
Prentice-Hall, Inc., Englewood Cliffs, NJ, 1974.

10. Gendlin, Eugene T., FOCUSING, Bantam New Age Book, 1981

11. Roberts, Jane THE FURTHER EDUCATION OF OVERSOUL 7 ,
    Prentice-Hall, Inc., Englewood Cliffs, NJ, 1979

12. Rozman, Debora, MEDITATION WITH CHILDREN, Univ. of Trees, Box
    66, Boulder Creek, CA., 1975.

APPENDIX A: CONSCIOUSNESS EXPANSION EXERCISES: Creating a More Harmonious Reality

Before beginning each exercise, close your eyes, take three deep breaths, and deeply relax. Visualize a calm, pool of water with no ripples, or your favorite scene in nature. Do this for at least one full minute.

1.   SENOI DREAM SYMBOL INTERPRETATION EXERCISE (Use also for unusual daily events, particularly coincidences and accidents.)

a.   Figure out the dream key (or symbols with the heaviest "charge"). Now see your dream key or symbol clearly in the center of your forehead, (one symbol at a time).
b.   Ask it, "How may I help you?" Now watch carefully. The image may change or you may hear words. These may present as intuitive flashes.
c.   Finally, ask, "Have you a gift for me?" Draw this gift immediately. As you draw it, more comprehensive understandings or reflections may occur to you.

2.   HOT AIR BALLOON EXERCISE (Use to identify and actualize priorities in terms of relationships or goals.)

Visualize a vast hillside with lovely, rolling green grass that has many bright wildflowers in it. There are many hues of reds, blues, yellows and pinks. (Pause five seconds) As you walk down the hillside, feeling the fresh green grass between your toes, you see a hot air balloon anchored in the valley below. It can be of your own creation and favorite color, or it may be rainbow colored, or with colors swirling. You are very curious so you hurry toward it. (Pause five seconds) As you approach it, you notice it is anchored with several rocks and on each rock is some writing.

This hot air balloon represents one of your special goals. As you walk around the balloon, carefully turn over each rock and read what is written there. Remember how many rocks you turned over and what the messages were. Now decide what to do with the rocks in order to take off in your hot air balloon to actualize your goal. (Responses vary. Some throw the rocks inside the balloon and take off, some cut the rocks free and some do not take off.)

GOLDEN DREAM EXERCISE. (Brings instant inner peace and release from daily problems while making a powerful energy thrust to materialize a wish or new probability.)

Visualize what would make you the happiest person in the world in great detail. Who are you with? Where are you? What can you see, hear, touch , taste or smell? Now see this event fully accomplished   and revel in it. Throw your energy into it and fully enjoy experiencing it. Really live it up! Note your body responses.

GOLDEN LIGHT EXERCISE. (Use daily for quick recentering and awareness of THE God within self and in others. It is excellent for small children.)

Imagine a great ball of energy coming down out of the sky. Now feel it enter the top of your head and go down your spine. (Pause five seconds).

Now feel this super brilliant light spread throughout your entire body into your arms and legs. (Pause five seconds).

Now let this great energy reach out to enfold everyone in this room, to bathe them lovingly in your shining light.

Let's remember this feeling as we return to the here and now, feeling peaceful, calm rested and alert.

RESOURCE BOOKS: Metaphysical Messages for Children Nine to Ninety

1.   Roberts, Jane, EMIR'S EDUCATION IN THE PROPER USE OF MAGIC POWERS, Delacorte Press, New York N.Y., 1979.

2. Bach, Richard, JONATHAN LIVINGSTON SEAGULL, MacMillan Co., New York, N.Y., 1970.

3. Burnett, Frances H., THE SECRET GARDEN, Dell Yearling, 1 Dag Hammerskjold Plaza, New York, N.Y. 10177 (14th Printing).

4. L'Engle, Madeline A SWIFTLY TILTING PLANET, Farrar, Strauss & Giraux, New York, N.Y. 1978.

5. L'Engle, Madeline, A WRINKLE IN TIME, Aerial Books, New York, N.Y., 1962.

6. L'ENGLE, Madeline, THE YOUNG UNICORNS, Farrar, Strauss & Groux, New York, N.Y., 1972.

7.   Lindgren, Astrid, PIPPI LONGSTOCKINGS, Viking Press, New York, N.Y., 1950.

8. Dahl, Roald, CHARLIE AND THE CHOCOLATE FACTORY, Knopf, New York, N.Y., 1964.

9. Dahl, Roald, CHARLIE AND THE GREAT GLASS ELEVATOR, Knopf, New York, N.Y., 1972.

10. White, Elwyn B., CHARLOTTE'S WEB, Harper, New York, N.Y., 1952.

11. Thayer, Jane, GUS THE GHOST GOES TO MEXICO, Wm. Morrow & Co., New York, N.Y.

12. Snyder, Zilpha, UNTIL THE CELEBRATION, 1977; AND ALL BETWEEN, 1976; BELOW THE ROOT, 1975; THE TRUTH ABOUT STONE HOLLOW, 1974; WITCHES OF WORM, 1972; THE VELVET ROOM, 1971; The HEADLESS CUPID. 1971; THE CHANGELING. 1970; EYES IN THE FISHBOWL, 1968; THE EGYPT GAME, 1967; BLACK AND BLUE MAGIC, 1966, Athenum Pblshrs, New York, NY.

PSYCHIC INTUITION

Andrews, Ted. ANIMAL SPEAK: THE SPIRITUAL AND MAGICAL POWERS OF CREATURES GREAT A ND SMALL. St. Paul, MN: Llewellyn Publications, 1996.

Choquette, Sonia. THE WISE CHILD: A SPIRITUAL GUIDE TO NURRTURING YOUR CHILD'S INTUITION. New York: Three Rivers Press, 1994.

________THE PSYCHIC PATHWAY: A WORKBOOK FOR REAWAKENING THE VOICE OF THE SOUL. New York: Three Rivers Press, 1994.

Dennis, Caryl, with Parker Whitman. THE MILLENIUM CHILDREN: TALES OF THE SHIFT. Clearwater, FL: Rainbows Unlimited, 1997.

Goldman, Karen. ANGEL VOICES: THE ADVANCED HANDBOOK FOR ASPIRING ANGELS. New York: Simon and Schuster, 1993.

 Hurwitz, Sue. THE LIBRARY OF THE FIVE SENSES AND THE SIXTH SENSE: Intuition. Danbury, CT: Frank Watts, The Rosen Publishing Group Inc., 1998.

Powell, Dr. Tag, and Carol Howell Mills, ESP FOR KIDS: HOW TO DEVELOP YOUR CHILD'S PSYCHIC ABILITY. Key Largo, FL: Top of the Mountain, Publishing, 1993.

Sandoz-Merrill, Bobbie, IN THE PRESENCE OF HIGH BEINGS: WHAT DOLPHINS WANT YOU TO KNOW. Tulsa, OK: Council Oak Books.

Virtue, Doreen. ANGEL MEDICINE: HOW TO HEAL THE BODY AND MIND WITH THE HELP OF ANGELS. Santa Monica, CA: Hay House, 2004.

______HEALING WITH ANGELS: HOW THE ANGELS ACAN ASSIST YOU IN EVERY AREA OF YOUR LIFE. Santa Monica, Ca. Hay House, 1999.

______MESSAGES FROM YOUR ANGELS: WHAT YOUR ANGELS WANT YOU TO KNOW . Santa Monica, CA: Hay House,2002.

SPIRITUALITY

Hicks, Esther and Jerry and Abraham. SARA AND THE FOREVERNESS OF
FRIENDS OF A FEATHER: AN INSPIRED NAARRATIVE OF A CHLD'S
EXPERIENTIAL JOURNEY INTO THE KNOWINGNESS THAT ALL IS WELL.
San Antonio, TX: Abrahma-Hicks Publications, 1995.

Kryon, channeled by Lee Carroll, THE PARABLES OF KRYON. Carlsbad,
CA: Hay House, 1996.

Millman, Dan. QUEST FOR THE CRYSTAL CASTLE: A PEACEFUL WARRIOR CHILDREN'S
BOOK. Tiburon, CA. H.J. Kramer Inc., Starseed Press, 1984.

________.SACRED JOURNEY OF THE PEACEFUL WARRIOR. Tiburon, CA: H.J. Kramer Inc.,
1984

________.WAY OF THE PEACEFUL WARRIOR. Tiburon, CA: H.J. Kramer Inc., 1984.

Myss, Caroline, INVISIBLE ACTS OF POWER: PERSONAL ACTS THAT CREATE MIRACLES.
New York: Free Press, 2004

Redfield, James. THE CELESTINE PROPHECY: AN ADVENTURE. New York Warner Books,
1993.